JOY ELIZABETH

me too

OVERCOMING THE TRAUMA
OF SEXUAL ABUSE

LIFEWISE BOOKS

Me too
OVERCOMING THE TRAUMA OF SEXUAL ABUSE
BY JOY ELIZABETH HELLMANN

Disclaimer: Some names have been changed.

Published by:

⚙ LIFEWISE BOOKS

PO BOX 1072
Pinehurst, TX 77362
LifeWiseBooks.com

Cover Design and Interior Layout | Yvonne Parks | PearCreative.ca

To contact the author:
www.JoyElizabeth.org

ISBN (Print): 978-1-947279-40-7
ISBN (Ebook): 978-1-947279-41-4

DEDICATION

I dedicate this book to the thousands of sexual abuse victims who have suffered wounds from not being heard or understood. I dedicate it to those who were most certainly not believed, and the most tragic, not being protected. This is for those of you who have been violated through sex trafficking, by relatives, church members, leadership authorities, Satanic ritual abuses, or by total strangers. By His grace, I have cooperated with my most loving Savior who has been with me, guiding me to a completed healing in this area. I do believe He has completed this miraculous healing within me, and will do the same in you, which will be my deeper satisfaction, and weightier reward.

I pray He will bring His rays of light into any darkness of soul. I pray His Spirit of Healing into infected wounds while imparting the inspiration to proceed forward, in this, your unique journey. You are precious in His sight. He cares. He listens. He understands. He alone is the healing solution for our whole man (spirit, soul, body). He has an individual plan for your heart and recompense for your assaults. He wants to walk you out of the trauma and out of torment. His power is so much greater and His light so much brighter than any darkness you have experienced. I pray you experience His healing presence washing over every cell in your body as I share the secrets of my journey with you. In Jesus' name.

DEEPEST APPRECIATION AND THANKS

I would like to first thank my Savior, who is the Mighty Counselor, for His loving, healing, and faithful power in my life. He is my healer and has done oh so well, in this great task of saving me. He used a variety of methods, resources, counselors, and mentors to ensure healing and wholeness from sexual abuse. However, I know with certainty who was behind each face, each book, each tool. It was my beautiful, most loving friend, Jesus Christ.

If it wasn't for Jesus empowering those He strategically brought into my life, they would not have had the grace to walk me through such heartache. Because they had willing hearts and open minds, Jesus was able to flow through these individuals with miraculous power that only comes from Him. These rare ones are the heroes in my story. God uses people to heal people. Sometimes we need Jesus with skin on, so to speak, to get the job done.

I thank these brave, selfless individuals who cooperated with the Lord to bring about the healing I needed, to become the whole person I am today.

TABLE OF CONTENTS

INTRODUCTION

It has finally arrived! There is a move of God taking place in the world and in His church that is bringing a supernatural awareness of the prolonged and nightmarish issues of sexual abuse. This is happening prophetically and strategically by the grace and love of God. It's amazing to watch these God happenings unfold before our very eyes. I've asked myself the questions, "Is this for real? Can it be? After so many years of constant cover-up, now truth is being brought into the light. Are we finally being heard and taken seriously? Furthermore, are those in authority helping those who have been defenseless? Is awareness on the topic finally causing a monumental shift, sounding the alarm that sexual abuses have, and will forever be, inexcusable?"

I hear God answering with a resounding, "Yes, and this move is here to stay!"

In all of history, we have never seen a day such as this. It has finally arrived. Many hearts will experience long-awaited relief. Help is on the way! Don't give up, today is a new day. No more hopeless wishing. No more delay.

I desire to give you, precious survivor, a gift of wisdom, that will allow you to make some substantial shortcuts in your healing journey. Please keep the following in mind as you read: I have written every word of this book with love and compassion for those who have experienced sexual assault. You matter, your pain matters. I labor in love to show you this with my words. I want you to feel and experience the love you never imagined you would ever experience. It is only by God's grace that I have cooperated with Him. Jesus is a loving Savior who has been with me, guiding me to a completed healing in this area. I believe He is The Redeemer! I do believe He has completed this miraculous healing not just for me, but for you, survivor. You are the one I write my story for.

CHAPTER 1

choices

SALVATION

I was five years old living in Mobile, Alabama. One evening my dad and I were watching a biography of the life of Elvis Presley. While I was watching, I remember a strange compassion started to roll over my heart. I had never felt anything like it. I was filled with deep concern for Elvis' salvation. Strange, right? But this was just how it began. God used normal, ordinary happenings to reveal Himself to me. He was (and is) always speaking. This compassion did not let up. There was a beautiful presence that intensified, and continued to increase, as if to tell me I should go and be alone. So, I went into my bathroom where I stood overwhelmed with so much love, conviction, and reverential fear, though I did not know exactly why yet.

I was standing in the corner of that little bathroom when a dramatic scene began to unfold. The Spirit of God gave me one of my greatest gifts—an encounter with Jesus. He was indescribable love. I recognized immediately that I was a sinner in need of a Savior, but also that the choice was up to me. I knew I needed Him in this life as well as in the life to come. I thank God to this day for the awareness of the lost state I would be in without Him.

These scriptures explain exactly how I felt: "For I was born a sinner—yes, even from the moment my mother conceived me" (Psalm 51:5; NLT).

"For everyone has sinned; we all fall short of God's glorious standard. Yet God, in his grace, freely makes us right in his sight. He did this through Christ Jesus when he freed us from the penalty for our sins. People are made right with God when they believe that Jesus sacrificed his life, shedding his blood" (Romans 3:23-25; NLT).

In this moment, I knew Jesus was real. He was only love, and He loved me beyond my capacity to explain. I started to cry saying, "I want Jesus. I don't want to go to hell." I wanted others to know Jesus and didn't want them to go to hell either. This was an encounter with God. I now know that I was made aware of these truths by the Holy Spirit. Man can't impart these types of spiritual revelations.

I stood there sobbing as Jesus came to me. I could see Him clearly with my spiritual eyes and hear Him clearly with my spiritual ears. He was smiling and consoling me, with a love that only He possesses. Jesus said, "You don't have to go to hell. There is a hell, but you don't have to go there. There is a devil too, but you can choose me and belong to me".

I will never forget how He gave me this choice.

"Do you want to *choose* me?" He asked as if He had to have my consent.

This puzzled me because my answer was an adamant, "YES!" Somehow, I understood He already knew that, but it didn't stop Him from giving me the choice.

"You can live in Heaven with me forever and I will never leave you," He continued.

After a while, my dad came in to check on me asking why I was crying. I told him I was going to hell because I didn't know Jesus. He kept saying, "No, you're not. You have asked Jesus in your heart, so you belong to Him." But I knew I had not. It is wonderful that a child can tell the difference between really knowing the Lord or not by the power of the Holy Spirit as He reveals truth to them.

"Howbeit when he, the spirit of truth, is come, he will guide you into all truth: for he shall not speak of himself; but whatsoever he shall hear, that shall he speak: and he will show you things to come" (John 16:13 KJV).

I told my dad clearly that I never asked Jesus into my heart, so he led me in a prayer to receive Jesus. By the power of the Holy Spirit I believed, cried, repented, and then was fully satisfied about my eternal salvation. God loves revealing himself to His little children.

"But Jesus said, 'Suffer little children, and forbid them not, to come unto me: for such is the kingdom of heaven'" (Matthew 19:14 KJV).

At age five, I had a falling-in-love-with-Jesus experience that preserved the spirit part of me at that time. My soul was positively affected through this encounter, but my soul had a lot of growing to do.

SPIRIT, SOUL, AND BODY

My salvation experience remained the most important piece of my journey to freedom because, being so young at that time, I hadn't yet received the revelation of truth that we are all spiritual beings who have a soul and live in a body. Later in my adult life, this revelation became a game changer for me and a crucial point in understanding deliverance and healing from sexual abuse. I didn't know then that it was possible for my spirit to remain undefiled and preserved from all contamination from the abuse because I was born again and filled with the Spirit of God. My spirit was a new creature from the moment I chose Jesus and His salvation. My emotions (which are made up of memories and thought patterns) and body experienced the effects of the sexual assaults.

For the longest time, I could not tell which part of me was hurting. Was it only the emotional part of me or was it my body? Don't they both affect the other? I felt like I was split in three different pieces. My soul and body had compartments of pain and trauma of their own, while my spirit remained preserved. God wanted to make me whole, entire, complete, and sound. He wants this for all of us. God wants us to experience divine wholeness, while the enemy will always want the opposite. The enemy would love for us to be fragmented, dissociative beings, who are confused about our identities. The revelation of spirit, soul, and body would become a priority for me to understand in order to discern which part of me was hurting. I could then target the appropriate part with the medicine of God's Word.

Here is some encouragement from Jesus: "I have told you these things, so that in Me you may have [perfect] peace. In the world, you have tribulation and distress and suffering; but be courageous [be confident, undaunted, filled with joy]; I have overcome the world. [My conquest is accomplished, My victory abiding]" (John 16:32 AMP).

God's Word clearly teaches that each of us are one whole person made up of three distinct aspects of our being as expressed through our spirit, soul, and body. Very few Christians know this fundamental truth and are able to apply it to their daily lives. I certainly didn't.

"And the very God of peace sanctify you wholly; and I pray God your whole spirit and soul and body be preserved blameless unto the coming of our Lord Jesus Christ" (1 Thessalonians 5:23 KJV).

Just as God is a community of One revealed as Father, Son, and Holy Spirit; He created mankind in His image as triune beings. We each have a spirit, soul, and body. What an impossibility it is to attempt to describe such a great mystery! It is the integration of our whole self that is crucial to living a victorious life. Every born-again Christian has undergone complete inner transformation spiritually. Lack of knowledge on the topic causes confusion and people may become disillusioned. So many of us confuse the spirit with the soul and lump them together as one. They are not one, but they are inter-related aspects of our total human nature. Your spirit was totally changed at salvation. Upon making Jesus Christ your Lord, your spirit underwent an instant and complete transformation.

"Therefore, if any man be in Christ, he is a new creature: old things are passed away; behold, all things are become new" (2 Corinthians 5:17 KJV).

Notice how it doesn't say that all things *are* becoming new or *have the potential* of being new. This verse declares that old things "*have passed away*" and "*all things have become new.*" Both of these are past tense, as in they have already happened. Our spirits are completely new in Christ. There is an ongoing process for our souls called sanctification, which continues while we are still on this earth.

The Apostle Paul supported this as well when he said: "Not that I have already obtained it [this goal of being Christ-like] or have already been made perfect (or, complete), but I actively press on so that I may take hold of that [wholeness or completeness] for which Christ Jesus took hold of me and made me His own" (Philippians 3:12 AMP).

Sanctification is a lifelong journey as far as our souls are concerned. We can all become impatient at times when we don't see the inward realities of our salvation manifest in our natural bodies or minds quickly enough. Typically, your body and soul are both impacted by what happened at salvation, but initially, it is neither total, nor complete. However, this doesn't mean we have not received the inward transformation the Lord paid to give us. Knowing this important truth is meant to keep you encouraged in your process of sanctification. We must not make the mistake of expecting that our exterior lives (body and mind) are automatically and immediately brand-new. Our circumstances and patterns have to change by the power of God through His Word and Spirit. We co-labor with Him through the process.

We have to remember that the change took place in our spirits first and then continues as an ongoing process, working its way out into our souls and bodies. When the sanctification of our bodies or minds doesn't happen quickly enough, unbelief may try to take hold. Don't become disappointed or confused. As we study God's Word, believing, applying and appropriating His promises, breakthrough will come. Therefore, you must never look into the natural realm to validate a spiritual reality.

Just because you can't use your natural senses to taste, touch, feel, see, or hear spiritual realities, doesn't mean the spiritual realm (and all it contains) is not real and able to be experienced. This takes faith. "For we walk by faith and not by sight" (2 Corinthians 5:7 KJV).

Maybe you can relate to the courage necessary for this faith walk. One example of the process of sanctification can be explained this way. We read in God's Word that He wants us to have peace, but the reality is that sometimes we feel as if we have no peace. The way we agree with God and bring forth the manifestation of peace is to believe that what His Word says is absolute truth. So, when we know God has given us His own peace, we can be confident that we possess His peace in our spirits. We can then bring our minds into agreement with this truth by believing God's Word.

When our minds have been renewed through believing and accepting God's Word as supreme authority, they align with our spirits and the biggest battle has been won. It has been my experience that when our minds and spirits are in total agreement it enables the manifestation of our desired result. The Bible calls this "walking in the Spirit" vs. "walking in the flesh" (mere human effort).

It's surprisingly easy how this works. Be encouraged. God will teach you His way to renew your mind. He is committed to your process of healing. "[Inasmuch as we] refute arguments and theories and reasonings and every proud and lofty thing that sets itself up against the [true] knowledge of God; and we lead every thought and purpose away captive into the obedience of Christ (the Messiah, the Anointed One)" (2 Corinthians 10:5 AMPC).

God wants us to receive all the benefits His Son suffered, bled and died to give us. We apply this principle to all areas in which we are not experiencing the fruit of His Spirit, or the promises given to us in His Word; such as, physical and emotional healing. We have established that we renew our minds by believing God's Word. Sometimes, this looks contrary to what we may see externally, even though it is indeed a present spiritual reality.

The process of sanctification continues as we are made aware of our God-given privileges as daughters and sons of God. We believe by grace through faith. The truth is then manifested as we patiently trust in our faithful God. Scripture encourages us to imitate those who have experienced healing. "Imitate those who through faith and patience inherit the promises" (Hebrews 6:12b; MEV).

We must exercise the fruit of patience toward ourselves as we are being changed from glory to glory. Be very kind to yourself through this journey to wholeness. "And we all, who with unveiled faces contemplate the Lord's glory, are being transformed into his image with ever-increasing glory, which comes from the Lord, who is the Spirit" (2 Corinthians 3:18 NIV).

On the other hand, the supernatural flow of life from your spirit to the physical realm stops when your soul agrees with what your body is telling you (majority rules again) and is dominated by the natural realm. You cut yourself off from experiencing God's life in yourself when you align your soul with your natural senses instead of what you know to be true from God's Word. "Do not conform to the pattern of this world but be transformed by the renewing of your mind. Then you will be able to test and approve what God's will is—his good, pleasing and perfect will" (Romans 12:2 NIV).

This transformation happens and is in process as we learn how to allow the love of God to heal our wounds and brokenness in ways our limited human understanding cannot always grasp. In the meantime, James reminds us that we have been given the power and the ability to believe God's Word which will change us. "Receive with meekness the engrafted word, which is able to save your souls" (James 1:21b KJV).

Everything you'll ever need in your Christian life is already present in its entirety in your spirit. After being born again, the rest of your Christian life consists simply of receiving, renewing and releasing what has already been given. You aren't in the process of trying to get or earn anything from God. At this very moment, your born-again spirit is as perfect and complete as it will ever be throughout all eternity. You won't get a new one when you arrive in heaven. Neither will it need to be matured, completed, or cleaned up from any defilement down here on earth.

Your spirit is—right now—as perfect, mature, and complete as Jesus, himself. "It is because of Him you are in Christ Jesus, who became for us wisdom from God—that is, our righteousness, holiness [sanctification], and redemption" (1 Corinthians 1:30 NIV). "God made him who had no sin to be sin for us, so that in him we might become the righteousness of God" (2 Corinthians 5:21 NIV).

As you renew your mind and believe God's Word, your soul will line up in agreement with what has already transpired in your spirit. When your soul comes into alignment with what it sees in God's spiritual mirror, which is His Word, then what's already in your spirit releases into your soul and body. That's how you experience the benefits of your salvation outwardly. A wonderful truth we can stand on is found in the book of 1 John. "Herein is our love made perfect, that we may have boldness in the day of judgment: because as he is, so are we in this world" (1 John 4:17 KJV).

Our born-again spirits are just like Jesus right now. Believing this truth will produce much victory and joy.

Think of your spirit person as the parent force that needs to govern your soul and body. If God's Word says it, we choose to believe it, and then we discipline our souls and bodies to obey it by practicing Philemon 1:6 (KJV) which reads, "That the communication of thy faith may become effectual by the acknowledging of every good thing which is in you in Christ Jesus". When your spirit and soul agree, you experience the life of God. When your soul agrees with your spirit, that means two parts of your being are aligned against one. Since we have seen the majority rules, your soul and body will experience the life, victory, and power that is in your spirit.

CHAPTER 2

the war for my soul

SUPERNATURAL ENCOUNTERS

Sexual abuse committed against me started after my salvation. Some might think that is really odd. I do mean the same year, same age. It was as if the forces of both heaven and hell were pulling me in opposite directions. I was caught in the middle of a war. I was so in love with Jesus and knew He loved me, which brought a certain security to my heart that some sexual abuse victims may not have had. At night, after everyone was asleep and when all finally became quiet, I would sit up in my bed and talk to Jesus. I would see golden silhouettes of His presence and feel my room turn into electrical currents of His love. It was as if my room was filled with electricity. It was a burning, tangible love. It was Jesus. Jesus is love. So, what I felt was the very essence of His being. I was coming into direct contact with His amazing love and presence. I was able to easily trust him.

My entire being was aware of the fullness of Jesus. I would later learn that these visits are called encounters. The Lord was so precious to me, and what sweet memories I have of Him at this age. My relationship with Him was so intimate and so real. During these times, I also remember conflicting, and very different, spiritual experiences going on. I recall that I had horrible nightmares where the devil would pull me off my bed, mocking me in my sleep. He would sing the song "The Joy of the Lord is My Strength," in the creepiest voice you could ever imagine. I slept with my light on every night until I turned thirteen. I knew one of them would show up, be it God or the devil.

As young as I was, I understood what was going on in my spirit. There was a war between light and darkness, good and evil. I love the fact that Jesus helped me through this. I simply trusted Him. I do believe Jesus destroyed the works of the devil on the cross. I know now that just as we have to stand guard against sin, sickness, and poverty (or anything that attempts to sneak in and make us victims), we must stand our ground in faith from a position where we know we have been given the victory over the devil, who is defeated.

We must guard our inheritance as daughters and sons of God. We do have an enemy that tries to kill, steal, and destroy, but Jesus won our battles long ago. We simply enforce His victory. There is a difference between trying to gain victory versus guarding the victory we have already been given in Jesus' finished work. Of course, my five-year-old mind did not understand all of these details.

Jesus always made me feel loved, special, and important. I knew I was on God's side and He was going to help and protect me. One example of His protection is that He revealed Himself to me and saved me before the abuse started. I can't imagine what would have happened to my spirit if it wasn't filled with Jesus before all the abuse began. God moved in at a strategic point of time in my life, so He could be one in spirit with me, preserving the most important part of my being. Who knows what would have happened to me if Jesus wasn't living in my heart at this time? "But he that is joined to the Lord is one spirit with Him" (1 Corinthians 6:17 KJV).

The consequences of any sexual abuse can be horrendous if not dealt with and healed. No matter how bad things are, there is always a good God at work, even when you can't see Him from your incomplete point of view. I encourage you to be open to His voice as He shows you areas where you may not have been aware of His presence. He will show you the whole picture. He will illuminate the places where He has guided, helped, and protected you with His faithful love. He was, and is, there for you.

SPIRIT OF TRUTH

God is the Spirit of Truth. Because He is who He is, He will enable you to face the truth head-on. He wants to set you free by way of His truth in every area of your life. Acknowledging the sins that were committed against you is a crucial part of your healing. There can be no excuse or deceiving yourself that something didn't happen when it did. I admit that it is still a bit of a challenge to this day to label facts as they were, using such strong language as "rape". Why can't we just call it "being molested"? That sounds a bit better, don't you think? Something in me would love to lessen the circumstances or at least minimize them a little. I will go further into proper definitions at the end of the book, but we must know God is with us on this healing journey and He gives us courage to face every adversary in truth.

Sometimes well-meaning people have said, "So you are healed? I bet you feel like it didn't even happen to you. I bet it's like it happened to another person". I wanted to say, "No, I do feel like it happened to me," and, "No, I don't feel like it happened to another person". That's the beauty of my story. There is plenty of grace for you and I to access in order to face our already defeated foes.

We must walk in the light of His truth. Denial of even the smallest of truths will not do. This denial does not please God or win you religious points. He does not condone such false suffering. In fact, sexual abuse is an area where people should be extremely cautious, knowing the enemy would like to hide and breed greater strongholds with us being totally unaware, which can keep a soul in utter bondage mentally and physically the rest of their lives, sadly never becoming free. "Be sober, be vigilant; because your adversary the devil, as a roaring lion, walketh about, seeking whom he may devour" (1 Peter 5:8 KJV). If allowed, the devil will attempt to take you where you do not want to go and keep you longer than you would ever want to stay.

Remember, Satan used God's Word against Jesus in the wilderness. Satan will attempt to use God's Word against you in the same manner. He used this trick on me many times. The suffering this caused was tremendous until I believed the truth of God's Word as it was intended. This is why understanding God's Word in its proper context is of extreme importance. One scripture I have seen the enemy use time and time again to keep victims in bondage is: "Most important of all, continue to show deep love for each other, for love covers a multitude of sins" (1 Peter 4:8; NLT). I know many people who have used this scripture to cover up sexual sin and abuse. This is error and distortion.

Don't let the enemy stay hidden and fester behind any religious facade that you are being more holy, or more loving by "covering another's sin". God will never use His Word to allow someone to continue to be sexually abused in order to protect the abuser. More people must become aware of God's true nature. God does not want abuse covered up. We need to be aware that this scripture has been used (along with others) to allow the enemy to do just that.

Jesus had to overcome the enemy by repeating God's Word back to him in proper context. The enemy said to Jesus, "If You are the Son of God, throw Yourself down. For it is written, 'He shall give His angels charge over you,' and, 'In *their* hands they shall bear you up, lest you dash your foot against a stone'" (Matthew 4:6 KJV). Satan looks to use God's Word against anyone he can, but God's Word is meant for your use against the enemy, not the other way around. Be aware. The war for our souls is real, but though the enemy uses sexual abuse as a tool for evil, God is much bigger. We can use God's Word to battle and gain the victory, experiencing healing and wholeness.

I believe the Lord has led you to read this book because He wants to comfort you. He wants to alleviate any emotional pain you may have from past abuse. My prayer is that you receive hope. Nothing is more powerful than a personal testimony from someone God has empowered to overcome their situation or circumstance. "And they overcame him by the blood of the Lamb, and by the word of their testimony; and they loved not their lives unto the death" (Revelation 12:10 KJV).

CHAPTER 3

my introduction to evil

CONFLICT OF THE KINGDOMS

I experienced poly-victimization, which is "...having experienced multiple victimizations of different kinds."[1] My spiritual term for this is "familiar spirits". I define the term familiar spirits as: demon spirits that attempt to re-victimize you throughout your life because they are familiar with the prior abuse in your life, and where they had access or entrance. Their goal is to make you a perpetual victim because you have been wounded and weakened in that particular area. Of course, God is all-powerful and you can be completely free of these spirits and patterns because The Mighty Counselor promises to lead you into all truth. He came to undo the works of the devil prevailing against such demonic entities. "The one who practices sin [separating himself from God, and offending Him by acts of disobedience, indifference, or rebellion] is of the devil [and takes his inner character and moral values from him, not God]; for the devil has sinned and violated God's law from the beginning. The Son of God appeared for this purpose, to destroy the works of the devil" (1 John 3:8 AMP).

MY FIRST TRAUMA

John, a young teenage boy from church, was raised by his single mother. My parents had them over to our house to counsel his mother. While my parents were counseling her, John took advantage of the situation. He did this through manipulation and lies I had never witnessed before. He knew what to say to my parents to win their trust in order to watch out for me while the parents talked. We were in a room close by, but this fact did not bother him at all. He was bold and confident that he wouldn't get caught. This was how crafty he was. He knew how long it would take for them to check in on us. He knew what to say to my dad to win his confidence. John took advantage of us all.

John knew everything about sex and taught me through physical examples. He coached me saying that this was what moms and dads did and it was normal. I was sickened, shocked, and full of shame. I felt contaminated. Merriam Webster's definition of contamination explains the feeling of it well: "The intrusion of or contact with dirt or foulness from an outside source."[2] My innocence was stolen. My innocence, "freedom from guilt or sin through being unacquainted with evil" was robbed from me.[3] Through this episode, I became introduced to evil. A healthy anger toward the enemy is still present for the years he tormented me with guilt. I didn't know guilt until this abuse happened. The enemy worked through this open door every day of my life until my deliverance years later.

GROUP ABUSE

Later that same year, I was walking in our neighborhood to visit one of my little girlfriends. On the way to see her, a group of teenage boys coaxed me over to their side of the street to talk. They were very nice to me. They asked me where I was going, and I gave them the little girl's name. They replied, "Oh, her brother is here. You can go see her in a little while."

They stood in front of some sort of shed. It had tools and yard stuff packed in it. Three of the boys guided me in while the other three blocked the door so I couldn't get out. I was violated by all three at once. Then they switched places and blocked the door to give the other three their turn with me. It was horrendous. They told me they would hurt my little brother if I told anyone. I knew they would because I had seen them picking on him before this happened.

This story is difficult for me to share. I was trapped, couldn't fight, and I felt powerless in every way imaginable. Looking back, I now recognize this traumatic event as the place I began to disassociate. I began to detach from all emotion. I remember I did not dare let any feelings of fear or disgust come up or out of me. I kept pushing my emotions down, so I could get through the abuse and get out of that horrible place. It was here that I first learned to comply in order to survive. Yes, survive. Because they were so much older and bigger than me, I was forced against personal desire to become as nice and cooperative as possible in order for them to let me go. They kept saying, "If you let us do this, we will let you go". I agreed unwillingly, only to get on their good side, so they would be kinder and gentler with me. The awful fear of dealing with so many of them at a time was horrendous…overwhelming.

The shame was crushing. My five-year-old mind didn't understand why they were laughing. They made fun of me while watching the person whose turn it was with me. I felt so devalued. They were laughing? I couldn't understand what was going on. I kept begging them to let me out of that shed. When they finally did, I just remember going home and forgetting all about it. I did not tell a soul because of their threats to hurt me and my brother. I knew how cruel they were, and I didn't want my brother hurt. I can only now explain the emotion.

I was a little girl. I wasn't thinking rationally or intelligently. It felt as though I was made to be less than human. How the enemy tries his best to strip us of any worth through such an evil event. But the enemy is a liar! No matter the assault, we have been redeemed and can walk into the reality of our redemption even if it is one step at a time. No matter what you have been through, there is a value, dignity, and worth placed upon your life by God, Himself.

I remember riding my bike one day after it had happened, and the oldest teenager started to come after me in the same manner he did before. However, a sweet lady was in her front yard and she saw me. I remember she began to scream at him to leave me alone and kept calling him a bully. She invited me into her house until it was safe to leave. She told me she had seen them tormenting me and told me to never go near them again. She would watch me as I rode my bike back home. I don't remember bringing it up or even thinking about it again until I was around thirteen. It was like I returned to my childhood self and had no thought or emotion about it.

MOST DIFFICULT ABUSE

At age six, my mother took my brother and I to her second cousin's house to babysit us. I had never met these cousins before. When I walked into the house, I was scared. There was an old lady with white hair sitting in the corner. Then, an eighteen-year-old girl came out to greet my mother, brother, and I. The girl was so friendly I felt assured everything would be okay. What I didn't know was she had an older brother who we didn't see until after my mother left.

As soon as my mother closed the door behind her, the events began happening again like clockwork. It was premeditated and planned. The young man took my hand and led me into his room and the young lady took my brother's hand and led him into her room. I remember not wanting to be separated from my brother. It's funny, my instincts told me what was about to happen because it had happened before though not with the same person. The young man was in his twenties. The things he did to me were worse than my previous experiences. He violated me for hours, in various ways. The abuse left me with physical and emotional repercussions that would last several years. I was baffled that he left the door wide open as he abused me. To my utter horror, his sister passed by and watched what was occurring off and on. Again, I found myself on display.

Several hours later, his sister came and took me to the store. She said she wanted to have some girl talk. I couldn't wait to get out of there. While I sat in the front seat of the car, she proceeded to ask me how my time with her disgusting brother was. I will never forget her evil, mocking tone and questions. She smiled from ear to ear as she told me she would buy me candy if I told her everything he did to me. I don't know what sort of sick, disgusting motive she had in her heart, but she kept pushing me for information. She knew I was violated and she wanted to hear the gory details.

I told her I didn't want any candy and I wasn't going to tell her anything. I thought about it, and then asked her if she would buy my brother some candy (my brother loved candy). I felt so responsible, that I should care for him. So, I asked if she would buy him some candy if I told her only one thing. She said, "Yes. I will buy him candy, but you have to talk and give me one detail."

So, I reluctantly, shamefully said, "He kissed me. Do you think he likes me?"

She said, "Yes. I know he likes you." She started laughing, continuing to probe. She took me back to the house and I gave my brother his candy.

These types of abuses happened off and on until I moved to another city when I was around seven. After the move, I could see how the effects of each trauma were showing up in my little life. But, I remained emotionally detached and clueless until years later.

CHAPTER 4

ongoing trauma

COPING WITH CONSEQUENCES

Two immediate consequences of the abuse I went through are particularly important to discuss at this point. Later in the book we will look at additional consequences that began to unfold and surface as I got older. The physical ramifications of abuse are many, but most of the time victims have not been educated at young ages. They don't know enough to understand or describe what's going on. They remain in the dark until later in life, oftentimes hidden away in fear and shame.

The physical pain I had as a child was excruciating. The physical symptoms came and went. I would be treated by a doctor with whatever medications he would give me to help, but the pain returned off and on for years. I remember being asked by the doctor what happened to me. I would always tell him nothing. I was truly paralyzed by fear because of abusers' threats, compelling me to be silent and to tell no one. That is what happens as part of this sick violation.

"Some physical symptoms are nonspecific such as dysuria, pain in the genital area, or blood in the underwear. Some are commonly associated with non-abusive etiologies, such as irritant vaginitis or urinary tract infections, and must be differentiated from child sexual abuse." [1]

Abusers not only violate the body, but also the soul to a deeper degree. This may manifest as emotional paralysis, which others cannot see. It is like putting a puzzle back together piece by piece. Only the Holy Spirit of Truth can help do this accurately. He is eager to help, though often others may not be. This blindness to the victims' pain leads to costly mistakes that continue to compound.

OBSESSIVE-COMPULSIVE DISORDERS

Sometime during my religious upbringing, I learned God's favorite number was seven. I don't know exactly how I came to this conclusion, nevertheless, I did. I started doing certain things in my daily routine seven times, so I would feel a connection to God. I remember the anxiety and fear of feeling incomplete until I did everything seven times. I hated getting ready for bed, because of all the rituals I created. But, the rituals made me feel secure. I would check out my window seven times, look under my bed seven times, check in my closet seven times, and say the same prayer to the Lord seven times. A false sense of security and completion would come over me and then I could go to sleep.

I now know that this was obsessive compulsive disorder (OCD). OCD is a mental disorder where people feel the need to check things repeatedly, perform certain routines repeatedly (rituals), or have certain thoughts repeatedly.[2] People who suffer from OCD are sometimes unable to control their thoughts or their activities for more than a short period of time. Common OCD activities include hand washing, counting of things, and checking to see if a door is locked. Some may have difficulty throwing things out. These activities occur to such a degree that the person's daily life is negatively affected. Often, they take up more than an hour a day. Most adults realize the behaviors do not make sense. OCD is associated with tics, anxiety disorder, and an increased risk of suicide. They often have endured child abuse or other stress-inducing trauma.

Honestly, I'm not into all the psychological terms for every disorder found. It seems as if there is always something new coming out and very few people can keep up with all the new terms unless you are in the medical field. Plus, it feels hopeless when people only label others, giving no answer or solution. It is as if they delete Jesus and His finished work on the cross from the equation. An individual can be free from *all* the effects of trauma through Jesus' redeeming love.

My point is this, no matter what the doctors say you have, Jesus is the Great Physician and will manifest healing in any area of need in your life from the traumas you have undergone. Your trauma was not greater than Jesus' power to redeem and heal. Remember He has come to bring us *abundant* life. "The thief comes only in order to steal and kill and destroy. I came that they may have and enjoy life, and have it in abundance (to the full, till it [b] overflows)" (John 10:10 AMPC).

I have both compassion for those who suffer and frustration with Obsessive-Compulsive Disorder. I fell prey to it like I was being fueled and controlled by a demonic spirit because the root of the trauma was not dealt with. The trauma was still alive and well, manifesting in various ways. I felt like it was taking advantage of my wounds to torment me further. It felt as though I came under a compulsion I couldn't control. The rituals varied from checking things repeatedly to spiritual rituals of constant prayers to be forgiven until I felt I did enough. Is it possible that some OCD issues are afflictions from the enemy, and if exposed, could be cast out? For me, the answer was yes.

Everyone is different and responds differently. This is my personal testimony. If you feel like this might apply to you, you have nothing to lose, my friend.

In Jesus' name, I pray His victory to heal be enforced in your life to free you from any strongholds where traumas first entered your life. But, by all means, don't obsess over this (smile). Let the Holy Spirit give you personal insight. "And I will give unto thee the keys of the kingdom of heaven: and whatsoever thou shalt bind on earth shall be bound in heaven: and whatsoever thou shalt loose on earth shall be loosed in heaven" (Matthew 16:19 KJV).

THE POWER OF BIBLICAL CONFESSION

It happens to be my personal observation that God has a unique plan on how He will set each person free. I pray this testimony ignites faith in your heart. At one point, while in prayer with some trusted leaders whose story I will share later in the book, I began to open and share my heart about the sins that were committed against me. This was a very real struggle for me, but they ministered to me through healing prayer and confession. "Confess to one another therefore your faults (your slips, your false steps, your offenses, your sins) and pray [also] for one another, that you may be healed and restored [to a spiritual tone of mind and heart]." (James 15:16 AMP).

I'm not saying that OCD is a sin you have committed. Rather, my opinion is that OCD can develop from trauma because of the sins committed *against* you. These sins committed against you may need to be confessed to a trusted pastor, counsellor or friend. This type of biblical confession was so liberating and healing for me. The reason we have used this scripture in its context is that we have so often only heard that we should confess our own sins, rather than any sins committed against us. Maybe seeing this scripture from this perspective can bring freedom in your life. The spirit that entered through my own trauma was dismantled with great ease.

CHAPTER 5

costly mistakes

IT IS A BIG DEAL

Minimizing is one of the costliest mistakes we can make about sexual abuse. If you think it's going to help the child or victim by trying to minimize what actually happened, it won't. In all probability, minimizing will have the opposite effect. The definition of minimizing according to Merriam Webster is to, "Underestimate intentionally: play down, soft pedal."[1] The excuses people give for not dealing with abuse properly are shocking. This mishandling or minimizing, in and of itself, is a destructive deception of Satan. Minimizing comments may sound like, "Oh, that's just kids being kids."

"Everyone has experienced that."

"That's no big deal."

"You made that up."

Oh, and my favorite, "You're too sensitive. Are you going to let this ruin the rest of your life?" I have even heard men blame victims because of what they wear.

Sometimes, the adult's behavior is followed by, "You never told us" or, "You told us too late". These responses do nothing but heap more blame on a confused and vulnerable child who is already dealing with the pain of shame. I have spoken to so many sexual abuse victims who have heard those words from adults. The adults attempt to sweep the abuse under the rug. This can be for many reasons. However, if it is in order to neglect responsibilities because the threat that exposure may make things messy for them; this is the height of selfishness.

In my case, minimizing the effects of abuse caused long-term issues as far as my value and self-worth was concerned. The Lord had to restore both over time, through a lengthy process. In some cases, minimizing abuse harms the child more than the actual abuse itself. Statements like those mentioned above reinforce the lies that the enemy is working hard to establish in a child's mind. Lies tell them that they have no value because no one believes them or is showing proper protection and anger towards perpetrators. This leaves the child open prey to more victimization. Years of unnecessary pain from trauma may be avoided if the event is handled in the godly, correct way with love and nurturing. The child/victim must feel open and free to express, with the appropriate persons, how the event(s) made them feel. The child must be safe to speak out no matter the cost to other individuals' comfort levels.

DENIAL

The reality of childhood sexual abuse makes people very uncomfortable. As you read previously, some adults minimize the accounts of their children because they think children are prone to exaggeration. Equally, adults in denial cannot accept that these horrific acts would ever be done by anyone within the family circle. Some parents carry their own history of childhood sexual abuse and are frozen in their ability to respond or take action. My own dear mother suffered terribly as a young adult from the effects of her own sexual abuse. Her mother was sexually abused, as was my great-grandmother. As a child I didn't know this. This wretched generational demon needed to be exposed, rejected and cast out. People do the best they are able until they have the proper knowledge to successfully stand against the insidious forces of darkness opposing them.

I remember telling my mother about different scenarios I was going through at age five. What I didn't know was that my mother was trying to survive her own terrible nightmares of abuse. Adding a victimized child to the dilemma was just too much. Can you imagine the pain of having to relive your own tragedy, and learning the horror of what you went through is happening to your child? People simply check out of reality to avoid the pain. This is common. People weren't created to endure such violation of body and soul.

Lack of acknowledgement set me up for years when I did not feel valued or worth anything. I would ask myself why my mother didn't care. *Why doesn't she believe me? Why isn't she doing anything to help me?* I felt so devalued, so worthless. Now, as a grown woman, I realize how much my mother deeply loved me. As you mature, you are able to look back and see the bigger picture of what everyone was going through in their own personal journey. People have different survival mechanisms and some are prone to fight while others are more prone to flight.

How wonderful it is that God has graced my mother and I and has restored years of cloudiness with clarity. The truth is that the enemy comes in and feeds you lie after lie in order to build strongholds inside you that he wants to use to torment you for the rest of your life.

Thankfully, my mother now understands how abandoned and rejected I felt. The pain this realization caused her was terrible. Nevertheless, these issues of perceived abandonment and rejection that I had were the most painful arrows from the enemy piercing my five-year-old heart. There is no easy answer. I have heard countless stories of parents, pastors, and school teachers who are so uncomfortable dealing with the issues of sexual abuse that children and teenagers remain victimized throughout their lifetime. That's just like the enemy to cover up truth and perpetuate the cycle of darkness. The truth is that sexual child abuse, in varying degrees of severity, exists worldwide.

COMFORT IS KEY

One of my most precious counselors told me that no one comes to her office if they've been comforted. Victims only arrive because they have not been. Sexual abuse victims need much comfort and consistent reassurance. This may feel like an unending task for those who are giving support to people who have survived abuse, but the Lord knows the sacrifice and will generously repay. This is one reason why God intended for children to be raised in a tribe. Children are meant to have many loving family members who help raise the child in love, a nurturing environment, and under proper protection. The two parents can't always provide everything a child needs, especially in these cases. We need solid family structures and support. Unfortunately, when comfort is not offered through compassionate listening and taking necessary actions to protect the child, many sad realities may take place. One of them being the child may continue to be victimized again and again. This causes continued mental, physical, and emotional ongoing cycles of trauma.

- "One in three women are survivors of sexual violence and one in six men are survivors of sexual violence.
- "Sixty percent of survivors are sexually assaulted by someone they know.

- "An American is sexually assaulted every 98 seconds.
- "Two out of three sexual assaults are not reported to the police.
- "For every 1,000 reported rapes, only six perpetrators will be incarcerated."[2]

CHAPTER 6

abuse and suicide

WANTING RELIEF

I believe God is merciful in bringing such a wakeup call on the topic of sexual abuse, exposing secrets that have been hidden far too long. Often, God Himself is used as the scapegoat by leaders manipulating scripture against their victims. God is allowing this wakeup call in the world and in the church by causing the hidden things to be brought into the light. There is, at present, a movement sweeping our nation, called "#metoo". I believe God desires us to raise our voices in unity. We are to stop these horrific cycles of sexual abuse, by bringing the issue out into the open; lifting up those weakened and oppressed.

For decades, far too many people in positions of authority, whether family, church or society, have allowed abuse to continue while turning blind eyes and ears. The strong should help the weak. Those who have power should help the powerless. Those in leadership positions should use their influence to help, assist, and believe those individuals who are struggling for their voices to be heard and to matter. It's hard enough just surviving sexual assault.

It is beyond comprehension that we add the grueling tasks of being your own defense attorney, pleading your case in an effort to help those in authority understand something they can't seem to grasp, unless they have experienced it personally. I have literally been told the following about an abuser who blamed the victim, "Sex is pleasurable. Why should the abuse cause a lifetime of problems if it wasn't your fault?" It was and is a scary and appalling statement, to say the least. The only sense I can make of it, is they have never experienced being forcefully violated.

Sexually abused children are violated in every possible way. Even so, the abused victims I've spoken to are some of the most patient, loving, sensitive, giving, sacrificial people you will ever meet. They can also be dissociative, prone to self-harm, and struggle regularly with suicidal thoughts or feelings. Survivors have told me the repercussions of trauma from childhood sexual abuse have caused ongoing obsessions with suicide and death when all they really want is to escape the pain. In fact, I have never met a childhood sexual abuse survivor who has not been suicidal at one point in their lives. This is not surprising. Inordinate pain (of any kind) and unabated trauma are primary factors in suicide. But why?

I was a very tender trusting child, very obedient. I learned the sad lesson that I could no longer trust everyone older than me. I had been lied to, threatened, and sworn to secrecy at the risk of someone I loved being hurt. My small body wasn't made for it. Plus, abusers program a child's thinking, manipulate situations, and train the child never to speak out or cry for fear of further harm. It felt to me like a no-win, powerless situation that was utterly terrifying. The child believes what he or she has been told, especially if they want to be "good", which was my obsession. I was made to feel at fault and responsible, but I couldn't tell you exactly the dynamics of how or why. Forget safety, control, or peace. Every day the child is on high-alert.

Childhood sexual abuse is perpetual trauma, which leads to many years (if not a lifetime) of sleepless nights, flashbacks, nightmares, body memories, or triggers that may send a survivor into a well of despair, physical pain, unrelenting panic, or terror. Anorexia or other eating disorders may be a coping response used by the victim to gain some kind of control over their world and feelings.

This trauma captures the brain. The adult who was a sexually abused child might still see the mirage of their abuser's face. The similar smell of the abuser's odor (shaving cream, cologne etc.) can send panic throughout the victim's body. The nature of trauma is the enemy's attempt to keep you imprisoned, shackled, remaining frozen in each memory from the violation. The enemy attempts to terrorize you with pain and fear, saying, "You need out. You can't handle this type of pain any longer. Just go ahead and die, no one will ever protect you. You don't even know how to protect yourself". This is his attempt to trap you into always feeling unsafe, utterly helpless and at the constant mercy of perpetrators. When those who should protect you turn a blind eye, this fear only compounds.

Those who survive the abuse and live to tell their truths and reclaim their bodies have strong, enduring wills. It takes tremendous courage and fortitude to do the work of dealing with the deep-seated memories, wounded emotions, intense trauma, unexpected betrayals, and to defuse the layers of terror. I believe you are reading this book because God has a plan for you and you will be one of the success stories. But unfortunately, some victims didn't know the Way out.

EXCRUCIATING PAIN

I once read a story of the assisted suicide of a young Dutch woman due to long-term childhood sexual abuse.[1] This woman in her twenties asked for, and was granted, euthanasia by lethal injection. She requested an end to her life due to intractable trauma (i.e., severe Post-Traumatic Stress Disorder) and concomitant medical issues (i.e., advanced anorexia, chronic depression and hallucinations) that left her primarily bedridden. According to the press reports, the young woman endured sexual abuse from the ages five to fifteen. She survived ten formative years of constant abuse. The doctors deemed her incurable, which is rare, and also speaks volumes about her deeply wounded state of being. This young woman sought professional help, but in her particular case, there was no lasting gain. She slipped further away, locked in a dark world of terror. [2]

I am sad for her pain and the suffering she endured. I have enormous compassion for this young woman. I remain angry that she felt so helpless and saddened by her final choice. This young woman was deceived into believing suicide was peace on her own terms. Her story is but one of many wanting relief, but not knowing how or from whom to get it. She, and her story, has made the world more aware of the severe, life-threatening trauma of childhood sexual abuse and the indelible marks it can leave on the psyche apart from Jesus.

I remember times during my own journey when the emotional pain would surface out of nowhere in dark waves of despair. All I could think of was that I wanted to die. When I had these feelings, I didn't want to kill myself, or ever thought of devising a plan, mainly because of my faith in the Lord. I knew my life was not my own to take. It belonged to God. Still, the pain was so deep at times. My emotions cried out for help, having never had the opportunity for healthy grieving. I was helpless. I didn't understand why or where these feelings were coming from. I had detached from the emotional part of pain in order to survive it at the time.

Sexual sin and its violations affect you differently until you allow Jesus to heal you. The following scripture passages show the magnitude of sexual sin: "All other sins a person commits are outside the body, but whoever sins sexually, sins against their own body" (1 Corinthians 6:18 AMP). "Whoever causes one of these little ones who believe in Me to sin, it would be better for him if a millstone were hung around his neck, and he were drowned in the depth of the sea" (Matthew 18:6 NKJV).

DISASSOCIATION

I had disassociated, which defined is, "any of a wide array of experiences from mild detachment from immediate surroundings to more severe detachment from physical and emotional experience."[3] I detached from the emotions. I was able to recall each scene but felt nothing emotionally. I was always able to recall each scenario of events about the abuse without any problem. However, I didn't feel the infected emotions until they came out of nowhere, when I least expected them. So, my feelings of pain told me something was wrong, but my mind couldn't put two and two together making any rational sense out of what I was experiencing.

CHAPTER 7

victory over demon spirits

THE BATTLE IS REAL

When you have a secure understanding of what it means to be born again, you are then able to understand without fear how the enemy can vex even a Christian in their soul or body, but never their spirit. When you are born again, no evil, no devil has access to your spirit man. You are a new creature in Christ Jesus, born of the Spirit, not of the flesh. "Therefore, if any man be in Christ, he is a new creature: old things are passed away; behold, all things are become new" (2 Corinthians 5:17 AMP). "That which is born of the flesh is flesh; and that which is born of the Spirit is spirit" (John 3:6 AMP).

Let me make it clear that these doors can be created by sins committed against you, or doors you open. Often times, we only focus on the sins we commit rather than sins committed against us. The good news is we have authority and power to shut these doors and never open them again. When caught and recognized, the demons using these doors to torment someone can easily be cast out and never return. I was shocked at how easily they left me (and never returned) once they were cast out through prayer.

Here is a passage of scripture that proves how a Christian may be demonically harassed or vexed: "And ought not this woman, being a daughter of Abraham, whom Satan hath bound, lo, these eighteen years, be loosed from this bond on the Sabbath day?" (Luke 14:16 KJV).

The proper term would be demonized, which is not an indicator of demon possession. The enemy is attracted to the wounded soul like a predator to wounded prey. These demonic entities, who are familiar with the traumas that have been inflicted, have access to the unprotected victim. They are then able to repeat the same scenarios and patterns until they are cast out. I believe these evil spirits latch on to the victim because the child is vulnerable, unable to handle such matters alone, and in many cases threatened to keep silent.

SILENCE

As we have learned, victims learn to be accommodating and most times keeps silent to prevent further harm. In my case, I felt responsible for the well-being of my brother and was terrified of further harm myself. Another reason for silence may be that the child senses the upheaval that speaking out causes in everyone. The pressure and shame they feel is more than they can handle, so they internalize the pain to avoid having to deal with it. The silence and darkness open many access points for the enemy. The enemy and his demons do everything possible to isolate the child in order to prevent the truth from coming out.

The enemy is crafty, subtle, feeds off secrets, lies, fear, and darkness. If he can keep the victim in the place of fear and darkness, he will at any cost. Remember, he's out to destroy God's masterpiece. The truth is, we have power over all the works of the devil, and that nothing shall by any means harm us. However, if the child isn't believed, prayed over, and allowed to get proper counseling, the enemy has access to continue victimizing.

THE PLAGUE OF FALSE RELIGIOUS ATTITUDES

I was a Christian abuse survivor. This added specific complications to my healing at first. I was a Christian but carried a tremendous burden of guilt. You could call it religious guilt or false guilt. One of the biggest challenges I faced in my healing journey was that I was a Christian and could not fathom why I still had so much pain. At this time in my journey, I was clueless in understanding spirit, soul, and body. The enemy used accusations and guilt to torment me. He would say, "Where's your peace? You're a Christian. Why aren't you victorious over your emotions? Why do you have so much pain if Jesus saved you?"

I was always so hard on myself. I tried to earn God's love by being as much like Him as possible. I felt like a walking contradiction. I was supposed to have righteousness, peace, and joy. But, during this time in my life, I was not aware of any. Where was the fruit? The condemnation I felt was excruciating. Honestly, it scared me because I knew I was supposed to have peace and joy because I had Jesus, but I was keenly aware of the absence of any wellbeing in my soul.

My name, Joy, added to the condemnation I felt and was a constant reminder of what I wasn't. I remember getting mad at God, asking Him, "Why would You do this? Why would You name me Joy? Is this a sick joke?" A lot of church folks made this worse. I wasn't joyful, but no one seemed to understand why. Guest speakers at the church would ask me to run around the church in front of the whole audience until, "I got joyful," or, "Broke out in joy." They would ask me, "Why aren't you smiling, your name is Joy?"

People kept telling me how I needed to become my name, Joy. There were prophecies about my name. Before my healing, rational thoughts never occurred to me. I never thought, *Oh, I ave experienced some traumatic abuses, so this is why I want to die and don't have joy.* No, my feelings were not clear or perfect, so I put them in a little box and set them aside to deal with in the proper time. I wasn't a crier either. It just added to the conflict pent up inside me. These feelings were separate from the thoughts. I know the lingo. Everyone says you feel what you've been thinking about, but it just wasn't true in my case. I wasn't thinking about anything, because I was detached from my emotions. My mind was blank.

The Lord had to educate me and integrate all parts of me: spirit, soul, and body. Again, this is one of the most confusing parts of healing to explain. It is perfectly normal for some of you to feel one thing with your emotions, think another thought with your mind, have perfect security in your spirit, but feel nothing at all in your body until the body memories start.

CHAPTER 8

phases of healing

FOUNDATIONS

By the time I reached the age of 21, I was aware of my dire need for radical change in my soul. I didn't know this at the time, but I had lost any value and respect for my body. This meant that if anyone touched me inappropriately, it was my "normal". I would shut down, turn into that five-year-old child, and survive. One example that comes to mind was when I was a little younger, taking a Driver's Ed. class with several other classmates at school. The Driver's Ed. teacher insisted on always buckling me up. He didn't do this to the other students, just me. He wouldn't allow me to put my own seatbelt on. He would purposefully graze my upper body with his body, taking advantage of the situation. Then as I was driving, he flirted and talked inappropriately to me in front of the other students. I thought, *Hey I'm just trying to learn how to drive and I'm nervous enough, already.* One girl in the car heard and saw this and reported it to a teacher, who then put a stop to it. If it wasn't for this teacher, who knows how long this would have gone on? I was still frozen in traumas of the past.

Years later, after God restored a healthy value for my body through healing prayers along with knowledge of proper boundaries, I understood what my vulnerable body went through. Repeated abuse held me in an emotional crisis, to say the least. The magnitude of this ongoing cycle had me trapped until I received the courage to turn to God. I had to learn to turn to Him concerning this taboo topic of sexual abuse. I learned to trust Him with the uncomfortable things.

God started showing me what to do to be free. He started to counsel me and give me what I would call precise, exact, instructions that were necessary to begin the process. I knew I had to cooperate with Him in the most surrendered way possible, or I wasn't going to make it out of the traps and patterns of despair. I had a reverential fear of the Lord in His inevitable process for my life, which is marvelous for maintaining obedience. He was loving and safe. I could trust Him. I learned that the eyes of my heart could look directly at Jesus, heart to heart, instead of being distracted by shame, pain, guilt, or sin.

The first thing He asked me to do was to shut myself in a room with zero distractions and read the books of Galatians and Romans. He told me to write these book passages out and to accept and believe them in a way that personalized them for me. He reminded me of my glorious childhood experiences with Him and that I must listen to His healing direction. He said to put first things first. He said I must know how I am saved. He told me that I didn't truly understand salvation and that we must start there. God knew that I had gone to a Bible school that did not teach that salvation came from believing in Jesus as Savior. They taught that you are saved only if you keep the rules, not if you believe and trust in the sacrifice of the finished work of Jesus on the cross. This, of course, is false teaching. Their teachings centered around good works saving mankind, which had nothing to do with His redeeming grace.

God wanted to teach me the full meaning of His good news and grace. I never wanted to study grace before, because I thought that I would become more sinful. The people who I saw preaching grace were often involved in immorality. So, I made an inner vow that I would not embrace grace. I didn't want to become like them (another trick of the enemy). It was in this context that God helped me understand that just because someone else had abused and twisted scripture, doesn't mean there isn't a proper use and context for our liberation as God intends it.

Looking back, I see how gracious the Lord was, taking me step by step. He led me as slowly as I needed to go, to ensure I had a solid foundation He could then build upon. During this two-year period, I didn't do much else. I barely left my home except to go to church or work (which was at the church). I was under strict discipline from the Lord to stay the course for my healing. It was as if I was in his incubator, kept from any relationships except for a few at church. It was here that he started to break unhealthy patterns, that had become habits, which would draw in wrong relationships. I was content with this process because the Lord was healing me. I could taste the joy and peace that I had so longed for, and I knew there was much more!

CHAPTER 9

God with skin

JUST THE RIGHT TIME

It wasn't until two years later that the next phase of my healing began. I was an administrator at a church, a worship leader, and the personal assistant to the pastor. I thought I was doing so well. I had been seeking the Lord for continued healing, but I didn't know what the more really entailed. Then, out of the blue, He brought two precious people, Wayne and Stephanie Boosahda, into my life, to help me on the journey of healing of sexual abuse.

Stephanie came to my church when I was 23 years old. I was an old soul, very mature and very put together, so I had been told. She was at my church ministering while the pastors were out of town on a month-long sabbatical. While she was there, it was my personal responsibility to care for Stephanie during her ministry. I picked her up for lunch one day. We were driving around and all of a sudden, she looked right through me. I could feel the presence of the Lord invade the car. She gently began to tell me about an impression she was having from the Holy Spirit concerning my life. With kind but piercing eyes, she turned and gazed at me, and asked a very delicate question. "Honey, have you ever been sexually abused?"

Without thinking I blurted out, "Yes, but I'm totally over it and I've never had a problem with it since."

She then said, "Well, that's good to know. But I sense there may be some deeper healing that needs to take place. If you are willing and open, Wayne and I would be glad to pray with you before we leave."

I agreed because I was always willing to cooperate with any part of the healing process in order to be free. I dropped them off for the night and headed home. It was like her words had located me and started affecting me in a very deep place. (This is just one reason why the gifts of the Spirit are so necessary and important. They can cut to the chase and save so much time in the healing process.)

My first thought was, *Lord, I'm doing okay. Don't stir anything up right now.* I had a few internal contradictions to deal with. This is a common conflict between spirit, soul, and body as you learn how to walk in the spirit. My second thoughts were, *Hope! Could this be it? Could they be the people God desires to use to bring my healing and deliverance?* My third thought was not as pleasant, *Is this another tactic of the enemy to use people to hurt me again?* I had to decide to cast all of the matter on to the Lord, letting it go completely, so as not to torment myself any longer.

At the close of their visit, Stephanie and Wayne prayed for me before I dropped them off at the airport. Their prayer for me was very long and detailed. I felt as if the prayer began to break up hardened ground in the soil of my heart. I remember the emotions that brewed inside me as God began a new work. When they flew home to Tulsa, I headed back to my house. I had no idea what awaited me or what healing really looked like. I didn't know what the process was going to cost me, but I was willing to submit to the Lord and do whatever it took to bring me freedom and get me to the other side. At that moment, I had to trust Him and take one day at a time.

BATTLING INNER DEMONS

I went about my daily responsibilities. While picking up the church mail, to my surprise, I had received a package from Stephanie. I returned to my church office and couldn't wait to open my package. I tore through it with extreme excitement but was totally shocked at what I saw. I looked down at a light pink, ceramic cross that had been designed to look broken into little pieces but glued together like a cross. On the back, she signed it. It read, "God puts the pieces of our heart back together." *Who is this woman? She has the nerve to send me a broken cross?* Of course, I did what any normal girl would do, I called my best friend. I laughed, and scoffed at that idea and asked my friend Karen on the phone, "Can you believe this? This lady Stephanie sent me a broken cross and told me God can put me back together again. Karen, she thinks I'm broken. Ha ha ha." I was still in so much denial.

Ironically, it was shortly after that when I began talking regularly on the phone with Stephanie. As I opened up, gradually my trust began to grow. When I was younger, I had wanted to belong to a Catholic church for the very purpose of being able to experience confession. I wanted to share the secrets of my heart, knowing the priest wasn't legally allowed to tell anyone what I confessed. Surprisingly, God granted my secret request for a safe place of confession in Stephanie and Wayne. "Delight yourself also in the Lord, and He will give you the desires and secret petitions of your heart" (Psalm 37:4 AMPC).

SOMETIMES YOU HAVE TO MOVE

Stephanie, Wayne and I talked off and on for about two years. She and her husband prayed for me and gave me counsel. I still didn't share the full extent of the details of my heart until I moved to their town near Tulsa, Oklahoma. Talk about a 'suddenly'. I never expected to move. Why would I want to? I had a secure job. I was doing a lot of good and working hard toward fulfilling my call. Then, God told me to go to Oklahoma. I can't even begin to paint the picture of how difficult it was, but I obeyed. I got in the car and drove sixteen hours. Mentally, I didn't understand what I was doing, but spiritually, I understood it completely. I was being led, driven out if you will, by the power of the Holy Spirit.

When I arrived at their home, the strangest thing happened. I got out of my car and walked up to their door. When I reached out to turn the doorknob, I heard the voice of God. He said very clearly, "Before you turn that knob and enter into this house, I want you to commit to Me that you will never tell them any lies. If you do, it will not only delay your healing, it will also have a negative effect on them. It's the truth that will set you free". The weightiness of God's voice was so heavy, yet tender and fatherly.

I wanted to ask, "Why didn't you ask for this commitment from me before I left and made this long journey?" But I knew Him, and He knew me. I understood I would have talked myself out of ever leaving and moving forward. His words located me, exposed my habits of lying to myself and others. I paused to think about what He said and what this commitment would cost me. I had been getting to know Wayne and Stephanie for the last several years. I grew to love and respect them dearly, and the last thing I would ever want to do is hurt them. After a few minutes of reflection, I told the Lord, "Yes, I will not tell them any lies". God got my full commitment. What a new pattern this was for me.

Oh, the grace of God that was on the three of us for this work of healing and deliverance. A divine miracle took place. All the pain started oozing out of my soul like an infection that had been neglected. God was causing it all to come to the surface, so He could remove it. I was incapacitated. It was like God waited all my life until this moment in time to let out the extent of the pain that was buried within. I was in a safe place, with safe people.

EMOTIONAL BLEEDING

I said earlier that I had dissociated. I could recall the events without the emotions attached to the abuse. Well, that all changed. I had the emotions now and without my consent. Emotions surfaced, and they were off the charts. I had zero control over them, which was a totally new experience. I sobbed and grieved with no end in sight. I truly didn't think I was capable of expelling such emotions. I started feeling every memory of abuse I had ever had.

Two things stood out that I didn't know were possible. First, I felt as if my heart was bleeding and I couldn't stop it. It was as if God was pulling back layers of indifference that had become permanent fixtures over my heart. Secondly, time just flew. It got away from me and it went by without my permission. I wanted it to stop and wait so I could get myself together, but I couldn't. The world and everything in it kept moving forward and it would not wait for me to catch up.

I was used to having my emotions under strict control. So, when all the wounded, vexed, tormented, emotions from tragedy erupted out of me, I was stunned at what had been trapped inside for so long. Every emotion from being held in that shed, everything that was said to me by my abusers, was up front and center. I was feeling raw, bloody and abandoned. I sobbed, wailed, shook, and screamed. I apologized millions of times for putting these two through so much, but they remained with me through it all.

They prayed over me morning, noon, and night. They walked me through every step of my deliverance. I couldn't even imagine how they were able to do all of it. We all knew it was God empowering us through the process. They encouraged me every step of the way...telling me I was most teachable and very obedient to whatever the Lord required of me.

Before we go any further, let me tell you about the kindness and graciousness of the Lord during this healing process. There were days when He would reveal things to me, instantly touch that area, and I would be soothed and made whole. Other days after praying, God seemed to want to do something else, and go in a different direction. I was truly on His watch, His time. Jesus was trying to teach me *patience in the process* for my healing.

Here's how I explain it. Pretend you make a trip to the doctor and scream out to him, "Doctor I can't take one more minute of this pain, so hand over the painkillers now!" He then assures you that soon you'll be over the sickness, but you must follow the directions on the bottle carefully. Then you get home and read the instructions that read, "Take two pills in the morning, two in the afternoon and two at night." You are absolutely appalled and start screaming on the inside, "I want to be rid of this torment now! Why can't I just take all the pills at once and be well instantly?" Well, more than likely it could kill you if you did that. Remember you didn't arrive at this place of pain overnight.

For me, God was dealing with nearly 15 years of mess. We must learn patience. The Lord is The Good Shepherd and He will lead you beside still waters instead of a raging sea, but it may take time. Surgery of the soul can be a timely procedure, but you can be okay with that. Why? Because you've been given a promise. "I am certain that God, who began the good work within you, will continue his work until it is finally finished on the day when Christ Jesus returns" (Philippians 1:6; NLT).

While my healing process was very intense from time to time, Stephanie had to teach me how to allow myself 'Seasons of Selah', in which to pause and reflect. She also emphasized the importance of rest and play as necessary. To her, play was always necessary. I had to learn to embrace the beauty of balance. Had I not incorporated this into this challenging season, I would have been completely overwhelmed.

Just like scuba divers that go to deep and dark places in the ocean, when it's time for them to come up to the surface, they have to take it very slowly in order to decompress from the pressure below.

If they ascend too rapidly, they will experience High Pressure Decompression Sickness, which can be extremely dangerous. There is such importance in the pace of healing. Much to my surprise, after only two days alone in my own apartment, I moved into Wayne and Stephanie's home. The pain when I was alone was unbearable, so they invited me to stay in their guest room. It was like the Lord planted me in a lovely garden that had light yellow wallpaper covered with dozens of roses. This room refreshed and replenished me from the inside out due to its beauty and calming effect.

Stephanie and I would wake up in the morning, grab a cup of coffee and be off to the porch swing with the two dogs, Nike and Lady. The backyard was a greenbelt of blossoming privet, and the fragrance ministered life back into us after the labor from giving birth to a new me. Some days we would do absolutely nothing except soak up life and play hard. I felt like I was caught up in a heavenly haven. Since I'd never been to a garage sale or flea market before, off we'd go to shop and she taught me the joy of 'making a deal'.

In the afternoon, all three of us would pray together seeking the Lord's face, inviting Him as the Great Physician to touch any broken places in my heart. He always did what He said He would do. At night we'd get 'take out' and then head straight to Blockbuster. We would leave there with an arm full of movies, comedies mostly. That would make us laugh and allow a merry heart to grab hold of us, which turned out to be medicine to our souls. The bottom line is that I learned the utmost importance of balancing work, worship, rest and play. God is a genius! He knows how to orchestrate our individual healing and it is so important to submit to His ways of doing things.

God has a perfect path for you to walk in your personal journey, too. In fact, God has a beautiful, individualized plan of healing for your life. Don't ever despair while reading someone else's testimony. Look to Jesus and say, "Me too! Lord, what You've done for them, You can do for me too!" The healing of the soul can be a great adventure, you never know who or how God is going to bring your life together for His ultimate purpose, but He does finish what He starts.

Be aware that at times, even other Christians can fire ammunition. Not everyone will be excited for your healing. There were a few people who didn't like the route God took me on for my healing. The very people you think will be in your corner, sometimes are not. Let it go and move forward. Give God time to work out all things for your good. Don't expect everyone to understand your journey. They don't need to. You have a responsibility to cooperate with the Lord for your own life. Jesus asks us to take up our cross and follow Him.

I remember a time I shared a little of my testimony with someone who helped sexually abused women. She literally got mad at me because of my testimony. She said, "You're lucky you had them [speaking about Wayne and Stephanie]. My girls don't have that option of someone praying for them." It really hurt me. I could understand where she was coming from, but the Lord reassured me He had (and has) a unique plan for everyone.

I can't tell you the countless number of people we offered the same Healer and healing to, who time after time rejected the healing process. It would start the same way it did with me. We met broken people who said they wanted and needed help for a variety of reasons. I assumed if others were given the same opportunity that I had, they would cooperate and receive in the same way I did. But this was not the case. We started noticing a pattern of "all talk, and no cooperation", which turned into draining, never-ending dilemmas with people who really don't want healing. It took me a long time to realize this fact. Just because *you* want it, doesn't mean *they* want it. This confused and hurt me greatly. I wanted them to experience the victory I had obtained, but the responsibility of choice is ours alone. Ultimately, God is the source of the healing. He is no respecter of persons and He will perform whatever miracle is necessary to manifest the healing you need. He has provided healing for us all, but we have to cooperate with Him.

CHAPTER 10

integration of soul and body

BECOMING WHOLE

After about two years of intense healing with Wayne and Stephanie, it seemed as though the need for the frequency of healing prayer lessened. God used them to establish a sense of true inward security that would forever keep me growing and help me remain on the right path toward healing. Through those two years, my mind and spirit seemed to align. I was no longer in the dark mentally and emotionally. I had experienced emotions from the memories of abuse, which were confessed, prayed over, dealt with and resolved. I had no more pain attached to the memories. I did, however, seek continued growth by finding

Christian counselors who continued to educate me concerning integration.

After experiencing so much healing in my emotions, it was now like I had two against one (spirit and mind unified) making it easy for the next part, the body, to be healed. The only thing was, I wasn't warned or prepared about this. I was a bit taken off guard, and fearful. I had no clue my body needed healing from memories until I started having some physical symptoms. Again, this is a common occurrence that sexual abuse victims encounter when they detach parts of their being from reality in order to cope and survive.

Again, I disassociated. When you disassociate, it's like your feelings get buried alive, but they are still living in you. They don't just go off somewhere on their own, never to resurface. These feelings must be brought into the light, expelled properly, then replaced with God's truth.

Mona first taught me how to do this. She was a wonderful, spirit-filled counselor. She knew the Lord and helped me know His love in a deeper way. I knew how much progress I made and never wanted lack of knowledge on a topic to surprise or shock me again. I wanted to work with the Lord and allow Him to continue the process of rebuilding me His way, built upon foundations of love and trust.

During this season of continued growth and learning about body memories (I had never heard the term), I discovered key answers to questions I had wondered about for years. I learned that part of the healing process is to have body memories. This simply means that while sharing your story you may shake or feel nauseous. Sometimes our feelings get buried alive because we didn't know what to do with them at the time of the abuse. God wants to heal those emotions and we need wisdom on how to properly express them; to give them a voice. You may have some physical symptoms while you're sharing these emotional events, but it's normal, and okay. Your body is detoxifying from all the poison that has been trapped in your soul for so long. The Holy Spirit will guide you into all truth and take each step with you. My body was trying to tell me something. I had to learn to become aware and to pay attention to my body's voice. Once I understood this, it really helped me to be gentle and kind to myself as I let my body respond how it needed to.

Every time I went into my counselor's office, my body would shake. It was okay because my body wanted to shake at five years old. I felt nauseous because I didn't allow myself to feel nauseous at five and six years of age. I felt fabulous when each session with my counselor was over. I felt such relief. I felt like emotions and complicated issues were being resolved. The fruit it bore was tremendously powerful and helped me to feel more secure about the healing process.

As I allowed this to happen, God was integrating my spirit, soul, and body back as one whole person. All parts of me learned to be present and aware. It felt like someone put me back together again, except way better than I was before. I learned how to value myself. I learned not only to value my voice, but also to value my body. I was giving myself value by allowing myself to talk, share and permit feelings to rise to the surface. Then the toxins would be surgically removed by Jesus, the Great Physician. I always saw it like a cancer of the soul that Jesus had to remove, and He did. As the Lord did this, the tangible peace I felt was more than enough to convince me I was on track.

A walk of faith is required for wholeness. It is of utmost importance to walk by faith with the Lord. You have to learn to trust Him. He created you and knows what you need more than you do. I loved the Lord and had a healthy reverential fear of how trustworthy He was. I knew He wanted my best. I also knew He called me to ministry and to be a part of His process to set captives free. There were many challenges to overcome and I felt at times like quitting the cooperation process, but somehow His Holy Spirit gave me the grace to yield and submit to each phase of the journey. This was not always fun, but it certainly was rewarding.

The Holy Spirit will always bring you back to square one, so you can have a firm foundation to stand upon, instead of falsehood that turns into sinking sand. He likes to start out in truth, no matter how hard that may be. He will give you the grace to accept the truth He reveals. With the truth set in place He may ask you to remain still; to marinate in it awhile so you won't forget it. Truth produces such peace. There is something about truth that will bring emotions of security. It's not that I always liked the truth that was revealed, but I knew if I accepted it, then Jesus could heal it and I would leave much stronger.

You can't progress forward while still stuck in denial. Somehow, the Holy Spirit made this crystal clear. The Holy Spirit teaches you, and the truth you now know will set you free. "And ye shall know the truth, and the truth shall make you free" (John 8:32 KJV). Acknowledging the truth takes back the control and breaks the demonic strongholds that have been created over time. It's okay to speak up and speak out. It's not easy at first, but soon you will experience the peace of His freedom that is worth it all!

In our sessions, Mona would ask me questions. If a bad memory came up, she would immediately invite Jesus into the scene saying, "Is Jesus there? What is He saying?"

My first response was a hilarious look back at her. "No! He's not there, and I wouldn't want Him there. Now ask me something else!" Truth. She was so patient with me. It took me quite some time, but finally, I allowed Jesus to come into each scene and be present.

I allowed His love and words to heal me. By God's love and grace, I began to develop new patterns. I got used to allowing the Lord to bring up different painful scenes from my childhood. I invited Him into those exact moments in time to literally feel the emotions that I had not felt at the ages when I was abused. Of course, it was embarrassing as an adult to realize how childish some of my survival mechanisms were, and to allow those same survival mechanisms to surface. It was especially difficult to voice them to someone else.

But the price of humbling oneself pays great dividends. I had to use this following scripture for encouragement daily. "Therefore, humble yourselves under the mighty hand of God, that He may exalt you in due time, casting all your care upon Him, for He cares for you" (1 Peter 5:6-7 NKJV). There were some days that were very challenging, but I learned that when I cooperated with the Lord, there was always payoff. "For to be carnally minded *is* death, but to be spiritually minded *is* life and peace" (Romans 8:6 NKJV).

In traumatic event sessions, there will be messages you will hear from both sides. The enemy is ready with his fiery darts and arrows filled with poison. They are aimed at you and his goal is to set up his strongholds for life, but his lying messages about the trauma must be recognized and rejected. Jesus is on the scene, ready to reveal the power of who He is. Jesus is ready with life-giving messages of love, protection and power to redeem and heal each painful scenario. As I listened to Jesus and His loving voice, rejecting everything to the contrary, all the physical symptoms of pain, nausea and shaking completely left. I never experienced them again.

I started experiencing His life and peace. It's funny how this works out, but it does. I found that when I cooperated and allowed the Lord to bring up different emotions to deal with, it was as if the next day He rewarded me with intense joy and peace of heart and mind. It was as if I had accomplished a great milestone. Because my internal reward was so rich and deep, I kept on the path.

He kept rewarding me during the process with the peace, love, security and joy that come solely from Him. He is working in us all, producing His fruit in our lives. "But the fruit of the Spirit is love, joy, peace, longsuffering, kindness, goodness, faithfulness, gentleness, self-control" (Galatians 5:22-23 NKJV).

Remember, Jesus wants your wholeness more than you do. He understands your specific trauma and pain and He wants to bring you total victory and relief. He is worthy to be trusted with your heart. He created it and knows how to handle it with such delicacy. He is the only one who can understand your inner world perfectly. Allow Him to show you this about His nature. It will bring you much resolve. "For we do not have a High Priest who is unable to understand *and* sympathize *and* have a shared feeling with our weaknesses *and* infirmities *and* liability to the assaults of temptation, but One Who has been tempted in every respect as we are, yet without sinning" (Hebrews 4:15 AMP).

He understands our suffering. Can you imagine this wonderful God leaving His throne, putting on weak human flesh in order to redeem us, all just so He can experience, share, know, and understand how we suffer? Jesus knows what it feels like to suffer mentally and emotionally.

Remember the crown of thorns placed on Jesus' head? The crown of thorns was used to make His suffering even more violent and painful, but I think it represents even more than that. "[The soldiers] stripped him and put a scarlet robe on him and then twisted together a crown of thorns and set it on his head. They put a staff in his right hand and knelt in front of him and mocked him. 'Hail, king of the Jews!' they said. They spit on him and took the staff and struck him on the head again and again. Jesus was then beaten by the Roman soldiers. In mockery, they dressed Him in what was probably the cloak of a Roman officer, which was colored dark purple or scarlet" (Matthew 27:30 NIV).

I've heard it said that the thorns in this "crown" may have each been one to two inches long. The gospels state that the Roman soldiers continued to beat Jesus on the head. The blows would have driven the thorns into the scalp (one of the most vascular areas of the body) and forehead causing severe bleeding. This event has a special place in my heart. It depicts exactly how Jesus understands the pain and anguish of the soul like no other.

CHAPTER 11

facades of forgiveness

FORGIVENESS TAKES JESUS

The subject of forgiveness can be quite conflicting and confusing to understand. At times, forgiveness can be complicated. Jesus doesn't want that for you. I want you to know I'm not talking about the obvious and simple examples or situations that we (hopefully) already know how to forgive. Just to be clear, I'm not talking about when your husband promises to clean up the dishes after dinner, and just doesn't follow through, or you discover someone has been talking bad about you behind your back. I think we all know human nature and that we are capable of committing the very same sins and do at times. We extend mercy and forgiveness to others, knowing that soon, we will need the same in return. Of course, we need to have the Lord's assistance when we forgive even the smallest of offenses. Trying to forgive without His help is frustrating and impossible.

Let's address more complex and complicated issues on the topic of sexual abuse and sins committed against the body. These are not as easy to forgive. This type of forgiveness, most times, can't be done in 30 minutes; however, your will and decision to forgive can be accomplished in an instant by the grace of God. Walking out that forgiveness takes time. We all know forgiveness is something we should do and are told as Christians we must do. But can we really? Furthermore, what does true forgiveness look and feel like? And we might also ask, *What's in it for me?*

I pray the Lord will shed His light on this topic and answer questions you may have experienced some agitation over. I think the enemy has complicated matters as usual, hiding behind religious facades disguised as true forgiveness. In fact, his methods are quite flawed and false, leaving us feeling trapped. Let's look at some false facades of forgiveness that the enemy likes to masquerade behind. Once we see what he is up to, we can scratch these possibilities off our list, giving us some breathing room to truly forgive. Hopefully, this process of elimination will direct your heart into Jesus' way of true liberating forgiveness.

#1 The Fake Facade

You can't fake forgiveness. It won't work, and God can't work with anything fake. We must take the responsibility and own our stories. What was done to you was wrong and will always be wrong. You can't trick yourself into real healing by faking a pretend reality. You have to look reality in the face and acknowledge the truth. Only then can you truly forgive.

Forgiveness isn't real if it's not true and based on true facts. (I feel the need to mention that this doesn't apply to dear people who can't recall memories. I know there are a lot of you out there.) That's not the way we received forgiveness from God. We received forgiveness from Him by accepting the truth that we were sinners in need of a Savior. We believed in Jesus as our sin substitute.

I don't know about you, but I was always one to go into every detail of how wretched I was apart from Him. I didn't and don't like to cover sins I commit from Him. I have to bring them out into the open and trust in His love for me, which is so much greater. It's the same way with forgiving other people. We don't deny the sin committed against us. We acknowledge it to ourselves and God and then, we forgive truthfully with our will, by His grace.

#2 The Emotionless Facade

I was trapped in unforgiveness because I was, quite frankly, catatonic. I would not allow myself to feel, experience, or express anger, sadness or fear toward those who perpetrated and violated me. Neither did I allow such feelings toward those who allowed the abuse to happen. You may wonder why I didn't experience emotions. It was because of the false religious mindset I had formed over the years that emotions were sinful. Please don't make the same false religious mistake I did. This had to be the biggest reason I had problems forgiving. God created our emotions. We are fearfully and wonderfully made. We were created in His image. He designed us to have emotions and for them to serve us, while adding spice to our lives.

So, what does forgiveness feel like? Forgiveness will feel differently through each level of sanctification and maturity. Are godly emotions only to be "sugar and spice and everything nice?" Most of the time, we know the emotions we should have, like love and joy. But what about the ones never talked about, like anger and hate? I love the following scripture. "Love must be sincere. Hate what is evil; cling to what is good" (Romans 12:9 NIV). God gives us permission to hate what is evil. 2 Thessalonians 3:2-3 (NIV) reads, "Pray that we may be delivered from wicked and evil people, for not everyone has faith. But the Lord is faithful, and He will strengthen you and protect you from the evil one."

In order to properly reverence the Lord, we must hate evil. I had to learn to hate sexual abuse instead of remaining a victim. I learned to hate manipulation and demonic control. I had to learn to hate being used. I learned to hate the devil and his deceptive ways. I had to learn to hate lies. I learned to hate domestic abuse and child abuse. I hate poverty, sickness, disease. We must learn to hate these evils and not accept them as our norm. Don't learn to tolerate such destructive behaviors. Jesus died to free us and give us victory over such things.

My conversations with the Lord used to sound something like this.

The Lord: "I want you to accept the truth in order to truly forgive."

Me: "I don't want to accept this truth. Let's just pretend it wasn't a big deal because if I allow myself to accept the truth about what really happened, I'm going to get mad, angry and have really bad thoughts and emotions that aren't Christian."

Sound familiar? It should. This is a general tendency for Christians who want to remain in this emotionless facade.

#3 The False Religious Facade

My inward dialogue went something like this… "Oh, being a Christian has so many duties that I am not capable of fulfilling, like to forgive. But I must, or God will never forgive me." Next came a little sarcasm mixed with fear and performance. "Fine, I forgive everyone, Lord, I forgive everyone in Jesus' name. Now, please forgive me and keep me from going to hell."

Nice, right? Ok, so then I tried a different method of forgiveness. I knew God wouldn't forgive me unless I forgave first (so I thought). So, I decided to make myself the villain of all evil and see myself in the worst possible way so others would look better in my eyes.

Me: "That will definitely make forgiving others easier."

Through this false, religious facade of forgiveness, I had trained myself to value everyone else more than myself. Everyone else mattered more than I did. I developed a sincere self-hatred in order to keep the rule of "forgiveness". This, my friend, is not forgiveness. When you have to use different methods or tactics to conceal the truth about what someone did to you, it is not forgiveness. Forgiveness is only real when you forgive based on the truth. You can't delete or deny what has been done to you. You can't make yourself the Jesus substitute for someone else's sins against you.

Someone told me once that forgiveness meant that you forgive the sin against you and you also release the pain to Jesus. I wanted to hold on to my pain because pain had become my false badge of courage. I didn't want anyone to take it away from me. It was here that God taught me His way of true forgiveness—but it was a process.

When the Lord showed me that I was holding on to pain and that He wanted me to let my pain go, it was one of the hardest decisions I had to make. I believed that if I let go of my pain, I would be in danger of being slack and allowing someone to take advantage of me again. Distorted thoughts, fueled by the enemy, gripped my heart through fear. God lovingly revealed scenarios that really caused me pain in my life. Scenarios where I had not yet experienced the glorious freedom and power of forgiveness that He alone can give through a willing heart. In each memory, with Jesus by my side and in my heart, I trusted Him. And I trusted the process of cooperating with His divine enablement to forgive.

You'll never regret forgiving someone. None of us deserve mercy, but all of us have been given mercy. Forgiving an enemy becomes easier with a revelation of God's love for you personally—it did for me. Once I abandoned all the false facades of forgiveness, everything was so much easier. For me, it was important to have an understanding and revelation of the love of God. I realized in order to experience the freedom I needed from the effects of what I had been through, I had to let go of the pain, hurts, bitterness, and memories. It was of utmost importance for me to forgive others, letting them and the pain go into the hands of God. It's not just about forgiving because it is our Christian duty. It is for our freedom! Unforgiveness will devour you, robbing you of your life and joy.

God doesn't want you to remain crippled by what someone else did to you any longer. He longs for your freedom which enables you to truly love and be loved without fear. You cannot do this by yourself. Only Jesus through you can forgive your enemies. Don't rely on your efforts without Jesus. You won't get very far. But He, through you, can deliver you from all of your judgments, bitterness, anger and hurt that others have caused. As you release them into God's hands and ask Him to work His good and mercy in their lives, you will find yourself soaring free from pain and going to places of healing that you've never yet been. Prayers to begin the process of forgiveness are in back of the book.

CHAPTER 12

the great defender

No parent in this world is perfect, like no child in this world is perfect. Both make mistakes. Both have misunderstandings and faulty perceptions. There is and has been only one perfect person on this planet, only one Savior, Jesus Christ. Jesus is committed to defending you. He won't bail out on His job. He will never be intimidated by your enemies and abandon His promise of protecting you. He will never change His mind about defending you. He is the only one that will be consistent, one hundred percent of the time.

Here are two promises to hold on to: "For the mountains shall depart, and the hills be removed; but my kindness shall not depart from thee, neither shall the covenant of my peace and completeness be removed from you, saith the Lord that hath mercy on thee." (Isaiah 54:10 KJV). "When my father and my mother forsake me, then the Lord will take me up" (Psalm 27:10 AMP). What was done was wrong and will always be wrong. Joan Hunter, a healing evangelist, often says in her prayers for those with trauma that, "Jesus took all of our sin, and all of their sin and put it on the cross never to be held against them again" when they accept Jesus as Savior.

ABRAHAM AND SARAH

Even Abraham didn't protect his wife, Sarah, because he was afraid for his own life. Hello…No disrespect to Father Abraham, I'm just making a point that even great people make mistakes. God alone does not! Listen to this story:

> "And when he was about to enter into Egypt, he said to Sarai his wife, I know that you are beautiful to behold. So, when the Egyptians see you, they will say, 'This is his wife'; and they will kill me, but they will let you live. Say, I beg of you, that you are my sister, so that it may go well with me for your sake and my life will be spared because of you. And he treated Abram well for her sake; he acquired sheep, oxen, he-donkeys, menservants, maidservants, she-donkeys, and camels. But the Lord scourged Pharaoh and his household with serious plagues because of Sarai, Abram's wife. And Pharaoh

called Abram and said, 'What is this that you have done to me? Why did you not tell me that she was your wife? Why did you say, 'She is my sister, so that I took her to be my wife? Now then, here is your wife; take her and get away [from here]!' And Pharaoh commanded his men concerning him, and they brought him on his way with his wife and all that he had" (Genesis 12:11-13, 16-20 AMP).

Abraham didn't just do this one time. He did it twice. My goodness... God Himself defended Sarah both times. God will also defend you. I want to encourage you to feel empowered by God Himself to face the truth to walk through your journey of healing to the finish line. You can make it. You are an overcomer. You have made it this far. You are a survivor. Look at all the Lord has brought you through. You are still here. Go all the way with God and let Him take you all the way to full healing. He will reward you and repay you for every violation.

Human beings are all capable of great evil. The evil of doing nothing. These sins of omission seem to get by us all. We don't even address the fact that there are things we are supposed to do that we don't do. I have seen abused victims hold onto bitterness and unforgiveness turning into the very image of their abusers.

However, it is healthy and vital to acknowledge the truth about the mistakes your parents, authorities, or other leadership have made. God wants to take care of you and protect you whether you're a young girl or a middle-aged male. It doesn't matter what age or the stage you are in. God wants to recompense you. This is why it is so important to know where you are in your journey toward healing.

There are those of us who have to learn to hate what was done to us, which will bring out emotions that are very difficult to go through. However, we must go through the process in order to get to the other side and be freed from the very person who sinned against us. Jesus Himself will make this up to us. How? I think each "how" will be very personal. Remember, there is an internal life that people don't see. It can be full of hatred or misery or it can be full of pleasures that are at His right hand forevermore.

GOD'S ANTIDOTE TO SELF-PITY

Self-pity is, "Pity for oneself: especially a self-indulgent dwelling on one's own sorrows or misfortunes."[1] "The heart knows its own bitterness, and no stranger shares its joy." (Proverbs 14:10 AMP). When you go through trauma like this, one of the things that you must understand is that no one but Jesus can fully understand the totality of what you've been through. This scripture helped me accept this truth. I always wanted someone to understand the pain, the violation of it all. The truth is, they can't. Only Jesus can.

There are different types of people with different levels of capacity to care or not care for the human soul. I have met many types such as the minimizer and the exaggerator. When I concluded by the Holy Spirit that no one except Jesus knows, truly cares, and can heal what really happened, I was then greatly satisfied. I must admit there were times it would have been nice to have others in my life understand, but it is not necessary for me to continue onward and upward. We human beings can be quite fickle in our emotions. We can change from day to day, but "Jesus Christ is the same, yesterday, today and forever" (Hebrews 13:8 KJV).

He never changes His mind about you. He is the one who wants to step in and show you what true pity looks like. True pity comes from Him. True pity is very different from self-pity. Pity means, "To love, love deeply, have mercy, be compassionate, have tender affection, have compassion" (Pity; Blue Letter Bible).

I love His antidote for self-pity. "Like as a father pitieth his children, so the LORD pitieth them that fear him." (Psalm 103:13 KJV). God, our Father always has an antidote. I also appreciate this definition of antidote, "A remedy to counteract the effects of poison needed, the antidote for the snake's venom."[2] There is an antidote to this poison of self-pity. There is a cure.

MAKING AN EXCHANGE

In my healing journey, the Lord had to reveal areas to me where I had embraced and held onto self-pity as a comfort and self-protection mechanism. Self-pity would show up, but not in the obvious ways. Others may cry, manipulate, throw some sort of dramatic fit, but mine was different. Mine sounded more like this self-talk, *No one understands. No one cares. No one protects. No one defends. No one listens. No one helps.*

I wore this badge of self-pity like a medal of honor. Self-pity turned into pride for me, which said *I can handle everything by myself. I don't need anyone's help.* And this, in turn, resulted in a judgmental attitude towards people. Then God asked me to hand all self-protection patterns over to Him. I did not want to turn it over to Him. The self-pity guard was mine, it was earned, and I had learned to feel safe with it. It took me years to build what I thought were wonderful structures of protection. There was only one problem, God was not included! Little did I know that while I was building such a strong, lofty fortress to guard my heart, I left no room available for the only one who could truly protect it.

God took me through a process, teaching me through examples where He did protect me. It was like He opened a personal photo album of our relationship. What a sacred album. He took me back in my memory showing me pictures of instances where He did protect me. This won my trust once again. He is so patient with us through each process of growth. Through this time with Him, He reminded me of His great love for me. I yielded in faith and turned over my power to protect myself. This enabled me to fully receive Him as my protector. What a beautiful exchange! The survival mechanisms we have are sad. They promise so much but deceive us into blocking the very care the Lord wants to give.

SCRIPTURE SUPPORT

Here are three of God's antidotes which will heal and cure wrong belief systems that have poisoned our souls. God's Word is medicine and cannot return void without accomplishing that which He has sent it for.

In the Book of Isaiah, chapter 61 (AMP) reads like this: "To grant [consolation and joy] to those who mourn in Zion—to give them an ornament (a garland or diadem) of beauty instead of ashes, the oil of joy instead of mourning, the garment [expressive] of praise instead of a heavy, burdened, and failing spirit—that they may be called oaks of righteousness [lofty, strong, and magnificent, distinguished for uprightness, justice, and right standing with God], the planting of the Lord, that He may be glorified" (v. 3).

"Instead of your [former] shame ("a shameful thing that has been done to you, or a shameful deed you have done" —in the Hebrew meaning of this passage) you shall have a twofold recompense; instead of dishonor and reproach [your people] shall rejoice in their portion ("destiny" in the Hebrew language of the Old Testament). Therefore, in their land they shall possess double [what they had forfeited]; everlasting joy shall be theirs" (v. 7).

God is a God who is magnificent operating divine exchanges. He knows all your pain and shame. He knows every sin that has been done to you. It pleases Him when we come to Him with our bleeding wounds. Only He can heal and cure us.

"Thou shalt no more be termed Forsaken; neither shall thy land any more be termed desolate: but thou shalt be called Hephzibah, and thy land Beulah: for the LORD delighteth in thee, and thy land shall be married" (Isaiah 62:4 KJV).

JESUS HAS REDEEMED YOU

Redemption says God will restore you to the person He created you to be before the horrors of abuse began. You may not know yet who you would have been. I didn't, but we find out our true identity in this beautiful process of healing in God's Word. God can be very mysterious. Sometimes, we have to trust in His goodness, knowing He works all things together for our good because we love Him. As Jesus is, so are we in this world. Father loves us as much as His own son, Jesus. We are righteous and holy, set apart, a royal race. This is our righteousness. I had to learn to trust Him even though I didn't always have the understanding. He eventually unfolds most questions we may have, but the real question He's looking for us to answer is: Do you trust Me?

I didn't in some areas, so He was patient in walking me through until I learned that I could trust Him with even the most sensitive of matters. Matters of the heart can be quite complex, but He created our hearts; so, He knows them best. Jesus can restore you. Christ's redeeming sacrifice on the cross was complete. "But of him are ye in Christ Jesus, who of God is made unto us wisdom, and righteousness, and sanctification, and redemption" (1 Corinthians 1:30 KJV).

Redemption is: "A releasing affected by payment of ransom, redemption, deliverance; liberation procured by the payment of a ransom" (Redemption; Blue Letter Bible). Redemption frees from what harms!

CHAPTER 13

only the wounded qualify

PURPLE HEART OF COURAGE

A few chapters earlier, I explained how awesome God's revelatory gifts can be helpful, speeding up our healing process when we receive and comply with His instructions. The example when Stephanie had a "word of knowledge" to pinpoint that I did need healing from abuse, helped direct and keep me on the right path to wholeness. Prophecy is such a wonderful gift of the Spirit, given to all who desire, in order to build up, edify, encourage, and equip. Although completed manifestations of healing did take years, it was cut shorter and made easier by these prophetic gifts.

Another example from my life when I was led prophetically, I found myself compelled to watch military training documentaries; specifically, the grueling process of boot camp. I had never done this in my life. But, I began to study and continued to study this for quite some time. The recruits were challenged and stretched beyond their norm of physical, mental and emotional exertion that they were used to. They had the choice whether they would stay or not. Would they be stretched and increase their endurance, which would empower them to be more than they had ever been? Or, would they, because they were given the choice, ring the bell and go home? To stay and stick it out or to bail out and go home, that was their choice. How easy it is to stay in the same place physically, mentally and emotionally—the comfort zones of complacency.

Here's an example of how the prophetic gifts work: You may not understand with your rational mind why you feel led to do something in the moment, but you feel "led or compelled" by the Spirit of God that lives in you. You can hear His voice which causes His purposes to come to light, illuminating your heart. God loves to guide us in this journey and will use anything to get His love message across to heal our hearts.

I love the way He speaks through pictures. A lot of spiritual realities are mirrored in earthly realities. One day, I was pouring out my heart to the Lord while wondering about the duration of my healing progress. (I was extremely discouraged at the time and exasperated that I was still in process.) I asked the Lord,

"When will this be over? Why am I still dealing with these painful emotions?" According to my standards, mind you not His, I felt that I should be much further ahead.

Wounds take time to heal and a close relationship with the God who loves you deeply and sacrificially. He was constantly encouraging me. When I paid attention, I could see this fact in motion. He then gave me glorious insight into His perspective and how He saw me in my process of healing. I had no idea that God was about to give me an insight that would change my whole perspective concerning the progress of my healing.

God gave me a picture of a *Purple Heart* medal that He, Himself was pinning on me! He was doing it so very proudly, I might add. I started to sob because this changed my outlook on just how much He valued me, that I had stayed the course and survived. I had been severely wounded by sexual abuse, but He never let me give up! There were many times I wanted out. There were many times it felt too hard to endure the process of cooperation for healing. We all have days like this where we wonder, *When will this be over?*

Many times, I felt like the recruits I saw in the military documentaries. I thought I was ready to *ring that bell*. But because of God's faithfulness, He who began a good work in me, continually inspired me. He covered me with a constant supply of grace, empowering me to never give up. Surviving with patient endurance is important in its season and should not be underestimated. Anyone can give up and call it quits. But, when you've endured with the courageous heart that God has given you; when you face all the blows of defilement, abuse, neglect, or betrayal, my friend, that deserves an award. "And the God of all grace, who called you to His eternal glory in Christ, after you have suffered a little while, will Himself restore you and make you strong, firm and steadfast" (1 Peter 5:10 NIV).

His goal for you is to be a woman or man fully alive. He wants you to live awakened, creative, and enjoying who He has called you to be without restraints or restrictions. The suffering and glory of mere survival will come to an end. You will make it to the thriving seasons in His fullness, just as He intends. "For our light and momentary troubles are achieving for us an eternal glory that far outweighs them all. So, we fix our eyes not on what is seen, but on what is unseen, since what is seen is temporary, but what is unseen is eternal" (2 Corinthians 4:17-18 NIV).

"The *Purple Heart* is a United States military decoration awarded in the name of the President, to those wounded or killed while serving. *You only qualify if you've been wounded...*It differs from other military decorations in that a recommendation from a superior is not required, but rather individuals are entitled based on meeting certain criteria. Soldiers are eligible for this award as long as the injuries were received in combat and with the intention of inflicting harm on the opposing forces. The Purple Heart is not awarded for non-combat injuries, and commanders must [consider] the extent of enemy involvement in the wound."[1]

If you've been wounded in battle, through this war of sexual abuse, let me assure you...you qualify for God's Purple Heart! God wants to award you for your endurance, bravery, commitment to fight, courage and in spite of all the obstacles you have faced, you are still alive! By faith you can receive this Purple Heart of courage for yourself and never take it off. Let the forces of hell know you wear it bravely, proudly, and courageously. Show the enemy he lost the war against your life. You have gained much ground, never to be lost again. You are still here, and you're not going anywhere but forward with God!

LEARNING SEASONS OF HEALING

"To everything there is a season, and a time to every purpose under the heaven: A time to be born, and a time to die; A time to plant, and a time to pluck up that which is planted; A time to kill, and a time to heal; A time to break down, and a time to build up; A time to weep, and a time to laugh; A time to mourn, and a time to dance; A time to cast away stones, and a time to gather stones together; A time to embrace, and a time to refrain from embracing; A time to get, and a time to lose; A time to keep, and a time to cast away; A time to rend, and a time to sew; A time to keep silence, and a time to speak; A time to love, and a time to hate; A time of war, and a time of peace" (Ecclesiastes 3:1-8 AMP).

I had to learn how to mourn and grieve in order to receive healing, because this was postponed at the time of the abuse. I had to learn to let go and allow myself to weep over the fear, injustice, bitterness and poison of every violation. I literally had to learn how to hate evil and perversion which I really didn't have a clue how to do, until I was restored. I had to learn to hate the enemy with all his subtle craftiness, deception and lies; for all those times he tried to take me out! I had to learn to scatter stones by setting godly boundaries in my heart, so I could receive and maintain His healing, and avoid abusive, toxic people. I had to learn to tear away from every cycle of abuse and all of its multi-layered mentalities. I had to learn to cast away every thought pattern and emotion that was inspired by the devil or man that was not in line with who God said I was. I had to learn to speak up, stifling my voice no longer. Silence wasn't an option anymore. I was ensnared in that trap far too long.

I had to learn how to love what was good, pure, and right. I had to learn how to love and value my body, treating it as it was, His holy temple. All of this is a description of the process of tearing down and building up, which the Master Potter knows well. He alone knows how to mold you in the exact image He originally intended. "Come and let us return to the Lord, for He has torn so that He may heal us; He has stricken so that He may bind us up" (Hosea 6:1 AMP).

YOUR TURN

Do you still have the facade of a strong exterior, while filled with anguish from the reality of abuse you've still not dealt with? Do you rely on survival mechanisms that you are proud of, and even amazed to have? I've experienced all of these scenarios in different times of healing on my journey. Not that I've come close to perfection in each scenario of sanctification, but I have left those places of tragedy years ago. There is only One who gets the glory. His name is Jesus. No matter which season of life you are in, His ultimate goal is to lead you to the place where you can speak up, give and receive love, dance, laugh, have internal peace, embrace and be embraced. All because of His healing presence in your life.

Let's stop being afraid of the topic of sexual abuse and rape. All we want, as survivors, is to be listened to and believed. If someone wants to share their story with you, one of the most important things you can do is listen. People don't listen anymore. You don't have to say anything. This is not about you, this is about them. Show them value by listening. A survivor needs to hear themselves acknowledge the words of what happened to them. The greatest gift you can give them is to listen. They may still have family or friend connections, or guilt that they played a role in this horrible abuse.

If you are a survivor, I want to reassure you that your abuse is not your identity and it is most certainly not your fault. There is no person on earth who can protect you, defend you or believe in you like Jesus. He took our curse upon Himself. "Christ hath redeemed us from the curse of the law, being made a curse for us: for it is written, 'Cursed is everyone that hangeth on a tree'" (Galatians 3:13 AMP). You have a choice. It was not an easy journey through the grief process to recapture who I was before. When people have failed to protect you, know that you're not the only one who has been taken advantage of and left unprotected. Human beings, apart from Jesus, are very weak and make many mistakes. I stand before you today stronger than my abusers. Genesis 50:20 (AMP) reads, "But as for you, you meant evil against me; *but* God meant it for good, in order to bring it about as *it is* this day, to save many people alive."

The process of healing over sexual abuse isn't easy, but you must refuse to be a casualty of war. There is hope, there is a way out of the darkness. The process at times will be humbling due to systems and patterns that must be torn down in order to build the new; but the reward far outweighs the price of a purposeless life of continued pain. It is worth the reward. No more demons, no more guilt. No more hiding. No more evil foreboding or nightmares. I can promise you this because I survived it, walked through it, and have been on the other side of healing for many years now.

I know the One who made it happen for me was Jesus. He saved my life and freed me from every demonic influence of suicide, guilt, PTSD, familiar spirits that attempted to kill me through repeated sexual abuse, and much more that this book can't cover. It will cost you a commitment to the truth, the whole truth, which is something we all struggle with for various reasons. You may feel worthless or like you've only barely survived, but God says you are a warrior, a fighter, a champion! I want you to know, that if you're still reading this book, I am convinced that you're committed to your healing journey. You have chosen, like a soldier, not to quit and not to ring the bell. So, my friend, I stand at attention and...I salute you! God has your hand and He wants to have your heart. He wants to escort you all the way through, to your finish line.

vital prayers

SALVATION

Dear Lord Jesus,

I recognize my need for a Savior. I believe You left Your throne in heaven, to come to this earth, becoming fully human, while remaining fully God in order to save me. I believe You died on the cross, bearing in Your own body all my sins, nailing them to the tree. You became every sin I would ever commit; past, present, and future. You willingly gave up Your life for me. I believe You suffered, bled, and died on my behalf. I believe You rose on the third day, conquering death, securing my eternal salvation, and now You are seated at the right hand of the Father. I believe You will come again to receive me, knowing I will forever be with You in your Kingdom. I thank You that You are now my Lord and Savior living in me. I am Yours and You are mine.

In Jesus' name,

Amen.

PRAYER FOR THE INFILLING PRESENCE OF THE HOLY SPIRIT

Jesus,

You said You would send the Comforter to live in me, never leaving me. I thank You for the promised gift of the Holy Spirit. Thank You that I am never alone. I receive the Holy Spirit by faith, just as I did salvation. I desire and receive my prayer language that I may speak in tongues by the Spirit of God. Thank You for this power to speak directly to Your Spirit from my spirit. Thank You that now the Holy Spirit will pray mysteries, intercessions, praises that will grow, and build me up in my most holy faith. I believe what You say in your Word, "But ye, beloved, building up yourselves on your most holy faith, praying in the Holy Ghost" (Jude 1:20 KJV). "For anyone who speaks in a tongue does not speak to people but to God. Indeed, no one understands them; they utter mysteries by the Spirit" (1 Corinthians 14:2 NIV).

Thank You for filling me. In Jesus' name,

Amen.

PRAYER OF COMMITMENT TO
MY HEALING JOURNEY

Precious Lord Jesus,

I know You are inviting me on this healing journey, individualizing it just for me. I say yes to You. I receive You as the Mighty Counselor in my life. I will listen to You above all other voices, making You alone the King of My Heart. I realize You use people to speak through, but I only have one Savior, You. No one else will occupy Your place in my heart. Guide me, Dear Lord, through every scary, dark place, and show me You were there and that my pain broke Your heart because You care and love me so much. Heal me in every area of my mind, will, emotions, and body. Heal every memory, every diseased feeling of abuse. Heal me at the very cellular level, removing every trace of trauma. Fill these once occupied places of darkness with Your Holy Spirit. I believe You are more powerful than all the forces of hell and that You have conquered them on my behalf by Your holy blood You shed.

I humbly, gratefully receive the full redemption You paid to give me. In Jesus' name,

Amen.

PRAYER OF COMMITMENT TO THE TRUTH

Dear Lord Jesus,

It is so difficult at times to admit the raw truth of what was done to me. I pray for Your grace and power to enable me to face the whole truth with You by my side. Please keep me from any self-deception. Without Your divine enablement, I won't be able to remain in the truth and will certainly fail. I admit my utter dependence on You. I ask and trust You to keep me. I receive Your Holy Spirit of Truth, guiding me and preserving me in Your truth. Solidify Your truth in my heart and seal it with the fire of Your love.

In Jesus' name,

Amen.

PRAYER OF FORGIVENESS

Father, with my will, I choose to forgive (name each person the Holy Spirit shows you) and ask for Your empowerment to truly do so. I know that by the power of the Holy Spirit, Your love has been shed abroad in my heart, so Your love is in me to forgive. Thank You for the power to forgive (name those the Holy Spirit brings to your mind). I release them into Your hands. I let go of all hurt and the memories that have been living inside me. I let go of all bitterness, anger, and judgments that I've held in my heart and mind against them. I release them. I let them go into Your hands and I ask that You forgive them and work good and mercy in their lives as You have in mine.

Now, I declare by the authority and power of my Lord Jesus Christ—I am free from (name) and they are free from me because of what Jesus has done! What they did was wrong and will always be wrong, but I take their sins against me and put them on the Cross of Jesus, never to be held against them any longer. I thank You, my loving and healing Lord and Savior, that I am free!

In Jesus' name,

Amen!

PRAYER FOR HEALING OF TRAUMA EFFECTS

My Dear, Precious Loving Savior,

I now open myself to the presence, power and working of Your Holy Spirit within me in every aspect of my being. I ask for and receive, through faith and a thankful heart, Your healing love to restore health and wholeness in me. I receive it even at the deep cellular level where the traumatic effects of past abuses have negatively affected me. I declare and agree with You that Your healing power is actively working in and filling every cell in my body. Every cell in the emotional and memory functions of my brain, conscious and subconscious, and in every operation of my immune system and every organ in my body, You are there. Through the authority and victory of Christ's shed blood, wash through me now and cleanse me of all trauma effects and flood me with Your healing light that casts out all darkness.

In the authority of my Lord Jesus Christ, I renounce all evil spirits associated with the trauma of abuse and its' effects and negative patterns at every level of my being and I command you to leave me—now! Holy Spirit, fill in every place where spirits of trauma have affected me and kept me bound. I thank You and praise You with all my heart!

In Jesus' life-giving and mighty name,

Amen.

DAILY PRAYERS AND PRAISE FOR INFILLING OF JESUS' HEALING, LOVE AND FREEDOM

(You may pause after each line of the prayers to ponder, meditate, express thanks, worship and/or pray in tongues.)

Lord Jesus Christ, Son of God, thank You for filling me with Your life.

Lord Jesus Christ, Son of God, thank You for filling me with Your love.

Lord Jesus Christ, Son of God, thank You for filling me with Your power.

Lord Jesus Christ, Son of God, thank You for filling me with Your Spirit.

Lord Jesus Christ, Son of God, thank You for filling me with Your light.

Lord Jesus Christ, Son of God, thank You for filling me with Your peace.

Lord Jesus Christ, Son of God, thank You for filling me with Your healing.

Lord Jesus Christ, Son of God, thank You for filling me with Your purpose and Your presence.

Lord Jesus Christ, Son of God, thank You for filling me with a passion to know You, love You and serve You.

Lord Jesus Christ, Son of God, I praise You for who You are, for Your great love and mercy, for Your mighty works of healing and deliverance that freed me from my past, and for Your great goodness and glory.

I thank You. I love You, and I worship You, my beautiful and wonderful Lord and Redeemer!

ABOUT THE AUTHOR

Joy Elizabeth is an ordained minister with the Greenhouse Network of Churches International. She ministers as a prophetic messenger to those seeking an encouraging, comforting word from Jesus and to be built up. Since 2000, she has traveled and served in itinerant ministry teaching in women's meetings and conferences.

Joy's first mission and passion is to know Christ and to make Him known, with signs and wonders following. This conviction flows out of her deep desire to walk in intimacy with Him and help others do the same.

Her second mission, which flows out of the instruction the Lord gave her, is to alleviate pain in the lives of His children by demonstrating practical steps of deliverance as well as bringing healing to victims of sexual, physical and emotional abuse.

As a survivor of sexual abuse herself, Joy has pursued and received healing through partnering with the Lord and experiencing a deep work in her heart. Because of Jesus, she is no longer a victim of the enemies' tactics or trapped in a web of condemnation. Instead, she has a desire to comfort others with the same comfort she has received.

Much of her twenty-plus years in ministry have been spent as a messenger of God breaking people free from bondages, such as: victims' patterns, unhealed emotions, and the physical effects that abuse can have on the body. Joy holds a Bachelor's Degree in Theology, with concentrations in Pastoral Theology and Systematic/Historical Theology.

Joy resides in Austin, Texas where she is active in full-time ministry as a pastoral voice in the lives of many women.

www.joyelizabeth.org

HOW TO OFFER SUPPORT

Here are a few phrases you might consider when speaking to someone who has survived a sexual trauma.

- "I'm so sorry this happened to you.
- I believe you.
- This is not your fault.
- You're not alone. I'm here for you and I'm glad you told me.
- Nothing you did or could've done differently makes this your fault.
- The responsibility is on the person who hurt you.
- No one ever has the right to hurt you.
- I promise, you didn't ask for this.
- I know that it can feel like you did something wrong, but you didn't.
- It doesn't matter if you did or didn't _____. No one asks to be hurt in this way."[1]

HOTLINES AND RESOURCES

Rape, Abuse & Incest National Network Sexual Assault Hotline
1.800.656.4673 | www.rainn.org

National Child Abuse Hotline
1.800.422.4453 | www.childhelp.org

National Domestic Violence Hotline
1.800.799.7233 | www.ndvh.org

National Teen Dating Abuse Helpline
1.866.331.9474 | www.loveisrespect.org

RECOMMENDED RESOURCES

Joan Hunter – www.joanhunter.org

- *Healing the Heart* – book
- Close the Door to Stress and Trauma – CD/DVD

Bishop LaDonna Osborn – www.osborn.org

- Biblical Equality – CD/DVD
- The Redemption Series – DVD

Gilbert Bilezikian – https://goo.gl/RYQKUS

- *Community 101* – book

Andrew Womack – www.awmi.net

- *Spirit, Soul & Body* – book

DEFINITIONS[1]

Grooming: A process of identifying and engaging a child in sexual activity. It involves an imbalance of power and elements of coercion and manipulation. It involves motivation and intent to sexually exploit the child. It is a process of desensitization.

Illicit Sexual Behavior: Takes place between a legal adult and a child (less than 18 years of age). These sexual activities are intended to erotically arouse the legal adult, without consideration for the reactions or choices of the child. Behaviors that are sexually abusive often involve bodily contact, such as sexual kissing, touching, fondling of genitals, and oral, anal and vaginal intercourse. Behaviors may also be sexually abusive despite a lack of contact, such as genital exposure ("flashing"), verbal pressure for sex, and sexual exploitation for pornography or prostitution.

Inappropriate Activity: Behavior, often times sexual in nature, that is not suitable considering the relationship status. Inappropriate activity might take place between a college professor and a student, or a superior and his/her employee. It is generally used when referring to two consenting adults.

Inappropriate Contact: Touching or contact that is not suitable for a particular time and place. Often used to describe either workplace touching or extra-marital touching. This term should never be used to describe an adult touching a child.

Indecent Liberties: Engaging in any of the following acts with a child who is 14 or more years of age but less than 16 years of age: 1) Any lewd fondling or touching of the person of either the child or the offender, done or submitted to with the intent to arouse or to satisfy the sexual desires of either the child or the offender, or both; or, 2) Soliciting the child to engage in any lewd fondling or touching of the person of another with the intent to arouse or satisfy the sexual desires of the child, the offender or another.

Molestation: Commonly understood to be the act of an adult subjecting a child any type of sexual activity. Child molestation is a crime involving a range of indecent or sexual activities between an adult and a child.

Poly-victimization: Having experienced multiple victimizations of different kinds...rather than just multiple episodes of the same kind of victimization.

Rape: The penetration, no matter how slight, of the vagina or anus with any body part or object, or oral penetration by a sex organ of another person, without the consent of the victim.

Re-victimization: The instance of a victim of a crime being subjected to either the same or a different type of crime. Many victims suffer re-victimization by a different perpetrator within a short time frame.

Sexual Abuse: A general term used to describe the infliction of some sort of sexual activity upon a person who has not given consent or is incapable of giving such consent. This can be used to refer to sexual abuse of persons who are differently-abled, a child, mentally challenged or an elderly person.

ENDNOTES

CHAPTER 3

1. Poly-victimization – Victims of Crime. Retrieved from http://victimsofcrime.org/media/reporting-on-child-sexual-abuse/useful-definitions

2. Contaminated – Merriam Webster Online Dictionary. Retrieved from www.merriamwebster.com/contaminated

3. Innocence – Merriam Webster Online Dictionary. Retrieved from www.merriamwebster.com/innocence

CHAPTER 4

1. Common Signs of Abuse – Joyful Heart Foundation. Retrieved from www.joyfulheartfoundation.org/learn/sexual-assault-and-rape/about-issue/know-signs

2. Obsessive Compulsive Disorder (OCD). Merriam Webster Online Dictionary. Retrieved from https://www.merriam-webster.com/dictionary/obsessive-compulsive%20disorder

CHAPTER 5

1. Minimizing – Merriam Webster Online. Retrieved from https://www.merriam-webster.com/dictionary/minimizing

1. Statistics – The National Center for Victims of Crime. Retrieved from www.victimsofcrime.org/library/crime-information-and-statistics

CHAPTER 6

1. Payton, Matt (2016). Dutch Woman's Story. Retrieved from http://www.independent.co.uk/news/world/europe/sex-abuse-victim-in-her-20s-allowed-by-dutch-doctors-to-undergo-euthanasia-due-to-severe-ptsd-a7023666.htmlINDEPENDENT

2. Payton, Matt (2016). Dutch Woman's Story. Retrieved from http://www.independent.co.uk/news/world/europe/sex-abuse-victim-in-her-20s-allowed-by-dutch-doctors-to-undergo-euthanasia-due-to-severe-ptsd-a7023666.htmlINDEPENDENT

3. Disassociation – Wikipedia. Retrieved from https://en.wikipedia.org/wiki/Dissociation_(psychology)

CHAPTER 12

1. Self-Pity – Merriam Webster – retrieved from https://www.merriam-webster.com/dictionary/self-pity

2. Antidote - Merriam Webster – retrieved from https://www.merriam-webster.com/dictionary/antidote

CHAPTER 13

1. The Purple Heart – Wikipedia. Retrieved from https://en.wikipedia.org/wiki/The_Purple_Heart

SUPPORT SERVICES

Phrases of Support – Joyful Heart Foundation. Retrieved from www.joyfulheartfoundation.org/6-steps-to-support-a-survivor

DEFINITIONS

All definitions were retrieved from http://victimsofcrime.org/media/reporting-on-child-sexual-abuse/useful-definitions

WORK CITED

1. *Holy Bible.* Amplified Bible Version. The Lockman Foundation, 2015. F www.bible.com/versions/1588-amp-amplified-bible.

2. *Holy Bible.* Amplified Bible. Classic Edition. The Lockman Foundation, 2015. www.bible.com/versions/8-ampc-amplified-bible-classic-edition.

3. *Holy Bible.* King James Version. Crown Copyright, UK. www.bible.com/versions/1-kjv-king-james-version.

4. *Holy Bible.* King James Version. American Edition. American Bible Society, 2011. www.bible.com/versions/547-kjva-king-james-version-american-edition.

5. *Holy Bible.* Modern English Version. Military Bible Association, 2014. www.bible.com/versions/1171-mev-modern-english-version. Scripture taken from the Modern English Version. Copyright © 2014 by Military Bible Association. Used by permission. All rights reserved.

6. *Holy Bible.* New International Version. Biblica, n.d. www.bible.com/versions/111-niv-new-international-version.

7. *Holy Bible.* New Living Translation. Tyndale House Publishers, Inc., 2007. www.bible.com/versions/116-nlt-new-living-translation.

8. *Holy Bible.* New King James Version. Thomas Nelson Inc, 1982. www.bible.com/versions/114-nkjv-new-king-james-version.

9. *Pity.* The Blue Letter Bible. Retrieved 2017. www.blueletterbible.org.

10. *Antidote.* Merriam Webster. Retrieved 2017. www.merriam-webster.com/dictionary/antidote.

CHOICES